THE HOME DECORATOR SERIES

PAINT

TECHNIQUES

THE HOME DECORATOR SERIES

PAINT

TECHNIQUES

ANDREA SPENCER

Consultant: Graham Carr

CONRAN OCTOPUS

First published in 1986 by
Conran Octopus Limited
28-32 Shelton Street
London WC2 9PH

Editor Liz Wilhide
House Editor Sarah Bevan
Designer Alan Marshall
Picture research Nadine Bazar
Location research Lesley Davey
Production Jill Embleton

ISBN 1 85029 053 9

Typeset by SX Composing Ltd.

Printed and bound in Spain

CONTENTS

POWERFUL PAINT

The simplest and most economical way to transform your home is to paint it. Traditionally, paint has played a dual role – of decoration and protection. But while modern technology has ensured the continuing success of paint as a protective medium, the decorative element has been sadly neglected over the years.

Until relatively recently, decorating a room often just implied achieving an even, flat finish, with a single colour used to co-ordinate walls, plasterwork and woodwork. Even today by far the most popular solution is to paint everything white. Historically, this was not the case. Artists, with their appreciation of line, colour and form, inspired the great craftsmen of the past. Surfaces in the home were treated almost like blank canvases, with oil- and water-based paints handled like colours on a palette to alter proportions, simulate finishes and create atmosphere.

Today, a renewed interest in a whole range of crafts has brought about a revival of these versatile techniques. No longer the sole preserve of the professional practitioner, the mysteries of the art of paint finishes have gradually been unveiled. Suppliers have responded to the new demand by selling trade formulations over the retail counter. The secret is out: materials are inexpensive and readily available, and the techniques can be achieved by anyone who can follow simple instructions and wield a paintbrush.

While there will always be a place for special skills, a whole range of stunning effects is well within the capabilities of the amateur. All the decorative techniques suitable for the home decorator are explored in this book, each one fully explained in step-by-step instructions. Details are also given of the equipment required, including cheap alternatives.

But most importantly, there are ideas for using colour creatively, for disguise and illusion, for decorating floors, woodwork and furniture – everything, in fact, to make paint a positive design element in the home.

Paint is not just a cheap and easy way to decorate your home: cleverly handled, it can also be used to create a subtle and gorgeous backdrop that changes with the time of day and even with the season. In this west-facing sitting room, the colours in the paint effect glow and shimmer in the sunlight, and in the evening produce a warm and cosy atmosphere. The finish was achieved by allowing solvent to dilute paints of several colours: a white eggshell base coat was allowed to dry, then washed over with varnish well diluted with turpentine. Tubes of paint in yellow, bright red, umber, ochre and white were squeezed on to the surface and allowed to fall down the wall. Another diluted wash of turpentine was then applied, and a dry cloth used to soften the drips. Enhanced by furniture in glowing dark wood and by glossy-leaved plants, the paint finish becomes an ever-changing, richly colourful, and very individual backdrop.

UNDERSTANDING COLOUR

Understanding colour is the key to selecting paint for decorative purposes. Before you start looking at manufacturers' ranges, it is a good idea to have a basic grasp of colour theory – how colours are formulated and how they inter-relate. While this may sound complicated, in practice it involves no more than experimenting with a selection of ordinary artist's oil paints and watercolours. Use white and coloured backgrounds to try out different colour combinations; referring to a colour wheel may help you to understand the composition of different shades. The familiarity you will gain with the way colours behave is well worth the outlay of time and money.

You should also explore differences in transparency. All paint colours are produced by the reflection of light from particles of pigment suspended in a transparent medium. How dense these particles are determines whether the colour is opaque or translucent.

In opaque colours, particles of pigment are so dense that they produce a continuous film which effectively eliminates any trace of background. This is known as covering capacity. Theoretically, all opaque colours can be produced by mixing the three primary colours, red, yellow and blue. In practice, however, colours produced this way may not be as brilliant as ready-mixed colours available over the counter.

Many professional decorators believe that colour is at its best in a transparent state. You have only to look at the brilliance of a stained glass window to see colour in its purest form. In transparent colours, technically known as washes or glazes, the particles of pigment are diluted to such an extent in the medium that, when applied, part of the background shows through. In this way, light is not only reflected from the suspended particles but also from the underlying surface. With the application of successive layers of wash or glaze, the background colour is progressively modified and the surface achieves a much greater depth and character.

The colour wheel

For centuries the colour wheel has been the standard way of showing how primary and secondary colours relate to each other. The 'painter's' primaries are red, blue and yellow, shown on the internal circle. In theory, all colours are produced by combinations of these three. Secondary colours, shown on the outer ring, are produced when two primary colours are mixed together. Tertiary colours are produced by mixing two secondary colours together; russet and olive are examples. Black doesn't appear on the wheel, but is invaluable when mixing colours: black and yellow gives a pretty, unusual green, for example.

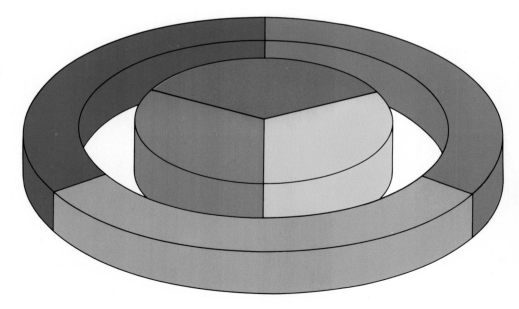

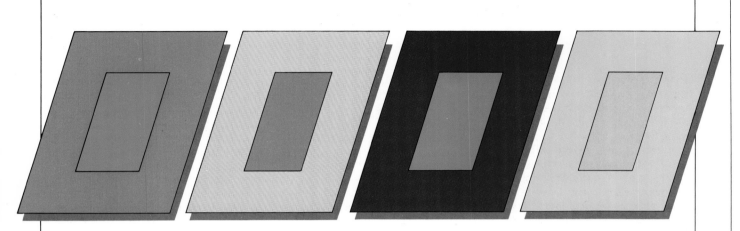

Complementary *colours appear opposite each other on the colour wheel. If converted into light beams and mingled, they will produce white light.*

Strickly speaking, a **tint** *results when white is added to a colour. The word is often used loosely to describe any shade of a colour.*

A **shade***, the opposite of a tint, is produced when black is added. In a decorative scheme, tints and shades of one colour can be used to great effect.*

A **tone** *is a lighter or darker version of the same colour. Colours with the same tonal value, as here, contain equal amounts of white or black.*

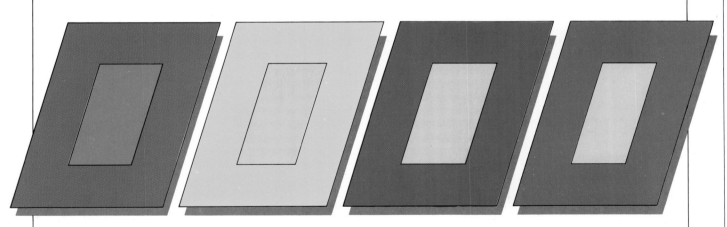

Some colours can send each other **off-hue** *when used next to each other: the result is a visual 'buzz', which can be very displeasing in a room.*

Discordant *colours have had their usual tonal relationship within the natural order of tone upset by the addition of white or black to one of them.*

Warm *colours tend towards red or yellow. An appreciation of the difference warm colours can make is essential when planning living areas.*

Cold *colours tend towards blue, and include some greens. Their effects can be restful and inviting or unwelcoming and, literally, cold.*

CHOOSING COLOUR

Colour creates atmosphere, style and character. It is the single most important element in any decorative scheme, but making a selection can be extremely difficult. For a fortunate few, the right choice is almost instinctive; others spend hours with colour cards, swatches and catalogues and end up more confused than when they started.

While personal taste does come into it, colours inspire certain common reactions which can provide a useful starting place. These responses derive in part from the natural world. Reds and yellows suggest activity and warmth; greens and blues are cool and peaceful.

But colour does not exist in isolation. Faced with a blank wall and a mosaic of colour cards, even a professional designer would be intimidated. Your choice should always be made in the context of the room you are going to decorate. Begin by taking a long, hard look at its inherent advantages and problems, paying special attention to architectural features, natural light and the use to which the room will be put. A thorough examination of all these aspects – good and bad – will go a long way towards suggesting a colour scheme:

- Does the room feel cramped or cavernous?
- Is it light and sunny, or dark and cold?
- Does it contain fine plasterwork or woodwork detail that could be accentuated?
- Are there any features that need to be camouflaged?

Below: The properties of warm and cold colours can be manipulated to good effect in decorative schemes, and tones and shades can be used to alter the apparent size and scale of a room. These four room sets show how the walls and ceiling seem to move in or out according to the colours used.

The colour and texture of furniture, curtains or flooring already installed in the room will also determine how you paint your walls.

When you have decided on a scheme, ask your local stockist for sample pots in the colours you have picked out (these will often be free if the supplier thinks you will return to buy the paint). Use the samples to paint a piece of hardboard or lining paper, position it in the room you are going to decorate and live with the colours for a while before finally making up your mind.

Special colours

If the right colour remains elusive, many stockists can mix up paint to your requirements. This service usually adds about 25 per cent to the price of a can but the expense and inconvenience can be well worth the effort. If you do have colours specially mixed, remember to note the exact formulation in case you need more later for touching up or for doing repair work on a damaged finish.

For the purist, there is no substitute for colour tinting using concentrated artist's colours ('tints' or 'stains') to mix up a special shade. With a little practice, this simple technique can be very rewarding, enabling you to produce a truly custom finish. Experiment first with small amounts, and follow the instructions on page 13.

Left and above: Nature can provide useful inspiration in your search for the right colour for your scheme. Time spent collecting samples in many different media will not be wasted, for it is only then that you see how colours work together – and how you react to the colours themselves.

THE MEDIUM

Paint comes in a huge range of quality and price. Always opt for the best you can afford: cheap paint is a false economy, for it covers badly and you will end up needing more.

Trade formulations are generally superior to common retail products, even though they are often more expensive. Previously available chiefly to professional decorators, such products as 'flat oil paint' and 'trade eggshell' have good covering capacities, flow well and are worth the extra cost. Non-drip paints are not suitable for the distressing techniques discussed in this book.

Types of paint
Most domestic paint consists of particles of pigment dispersed in a medium. The medium, which can be either oil or water, gives the paint certain fundamental characteristics, determining how it is thinned, its ease of application and drying time. Never mix the two types when wet – they are incompatible.

Oil-based: These paints are marginally more expensive than their water-based counterparts. They have a pungent odour, are relatively slow-drying and splashes may be difficult to remove. The solvent is white spirit. They can be applied over any painted surface that is dry, clean and grease-free. It is advisable to sand eggshell or gloss finishes lightly to provide a key for the next coat of paint.

Water-based: Commonly known as emulsion, water-based paints are popular for home decoration. Quick-drying, the solvent is water, which also makes clearing up easier. Ideally, they should be applied over water-based ground coats. If they are used over oil-based grounds, the surface must be clean, dry and grease-free.

Texture
Both main types of paint are available in a variety of finishes: matt, mid-sheen and gloss. Matt is best for large, flat areas, although if the surface is free of imperfections, mid-sheen can give a lustrous look. Gloss has traditionally been a popular

choice for woodwork but it can look sticky and overstated; mid-sheen is a more elegant treatment.

Thinning
As a rule two thin coats are better than one thick one, especially if the first coat is sanded down. Never thin non-drip paints. The thinner the paint, the faster it will dry – and the further it will go – but opacity will be sacrificed. When thinning opaque paints, it is important to follow the manufacturer's instructions. Thinning is one of the ways you create glazes and washes, which are central to most special paint techniques; in this case the paint is diluted to a considerable extent.

Tinting
Although modern colour ranges are fairly extensive, tinting may be the only way to get the exact shade you require. Tinters, either oil-based artist's oils or water-based artist's gouache, come in a vast range of colours which can be mixed or used on their own.

First, dissolve the tinter in a small amount of the appropriate solvent. Then, stirring continuously, add the tinter little by little to a base of white paint, or to a coloured paint if that is nearer to the shade you are trying to achieve. (Never use non-drip paints.) Experiment with different tints and amounts – but remember to note which you used and the quantities when you finally get the result you want.

Tints can be used on their own, suitably thinned, to pick out detail in plasterwork, woodwork or furniture. When thinned to transparency they can be used as colour washes.

Colour is not the only thing at your disposal when planning a decorative scheme. This picture shows how you can create drama simply by exploiting the texture of the paint itself, in this case by the use of gloss paint on the unpanelled doors.

FLAT COLOUR

There are many occasions when the honest simplicity of a flat colour scheme is the best solution. Plain backgrounds are even essential for certain rooms, where a more decorative treatment would be too hectic. If furnishings are heavily patterned, or the room teems with a profusion of brightly coloured objects, the walls should act as a backdrop and not compete for attention. A richly decorative effect can also be inappropriate in workrooms such as kitchens and studies, where the eye can easily be distracted. Rooms that feature a good deal of natural relief such as alcoves, recesses or beams, can also benefit from flat colour, to bring out the sculptural effect caused by the interplay of light and shade. Hallways, too, are good places for a neutral treatment, to make a smooth transition from one colour scheme to the next.

Whether your aim is to provide visual relief, or whether it is to be bold and emphatic, choice of colour is of the greatest importance. Lighten and enlarge small, dark rooms with pastel colours; draw in big spaces with warm mid-tones. High ceilings can be visually lowered if they are painted a shade darker than the walls; a shade lighter gives the opposite effect. Even white or neutral colours deserve careful consideration. It's a good idea, for example, to avoid the blue cast of 'brilliant white' if the room is already cool in tone. A trade formulation called 'pastel base', a soft white without the addition of pigment, makes an ideal base for tints. Adding small amounts of raw umber and raw sienna will create a rich, 'aged' white with a depth to it that is gentle on the eye.

You can add interest to a flat colour scheme by picking out decorative trim such as mouldings or cornices in different shades. This can also have the effect of adjusting the scale and proportion of a room. Painting picture rails, dados or skirting boards in a different colour, for example, would make a border for the walls and lower a high-ceilinged room. If you decide to adopt this approach, exercise some restraint – soft gradations of colour are more effective than loud contrasts.

Of all artistic movements, the Impressionist painters of the nineteenth century have had the greatest and most enduring influence on the way subsequent generations respond to the natural world. They not only understood but managed to transmit on to canvas the natural law that colour is a function of light. Claude Monet used the same principles when painting the interior of his house as when he painted his canvases: at Giverny he created a living environment steeped in colour and flooded with light. It is a fabulous illustration of the way one colour taken directly from nature – perhaps from daffodils, or from the sun itself – and used without timidity can be wholly sufficient as a decorative treatment.

Above: Flat colour can be used to good effect on features like these beams. China blue was chosen to pick up the colour in the plates, and it chimes harmoniously with the style of the house.

Right: Neutral colours in different tones and shades here create a calm and unobtrusive scheme that allows the kitchen range to be the focus of attention. A paper frieze provides inexpensive detail.

Above: There is so much interesting panelled wood in this room that simply painting it in a cool colour is sufficient to create a pleasing effect. The wood itself suggests warmth and domesticity, so there is no need to repeat the message with an elaborately cosy paint effect.

Left: A monochrome scheme can be more dramatic and meaningful than those using many colours. This kitchen speaks of the twentieth-century: cool, efficient modernity is implicit in every corner, and the normal clutter of daily life is made to look purposeful and workmanlike.

BROKEN COLOUR

Ranging in effect from subtle, delicately shaded backdrops to bold, dominant patterning, many broken colour techniques are simple, quick and inexpensive. And it's not just walls that can receive the treatment – floors, woodwork and even furniture can be decorated using the same methods.

All broken colour techniques involve the use of a broken film of paint in the form of a transparent glaze or wash applied over an opaque background. Depending on the method, an enormous range of colours, tones, textures and patterns can be created.

There are two main types of technique: additive and sub-tractive. In both cases, a white or coloured opaque ground is first applied to a suitably prepared surface and allowed to dry. Then a different colour is prepared, often thinned to transparency. In additive techniques, this colour is applied in a broken film. Where it is covered, the background is subtly modified. In subtractive techniques, a continuous film of the second colour is applied and then broken up, or 'distressed', to reveal the background. As before, where it is covered, the ground colour is subtly modified.

Tools range from conventional paintbrushes to marine sponges, rags, combs, sprays and even toothbrushes. All produce the highly recognizable signatures that are charac-teristic of broken colour. There is no limit to the number of layers that can be built up, provided each is allowed to dry before the next is applied.

Central to these techniques is the use of transparent glazes and washes. Although either can be used, each system has its own advantages. Glazes tend to be slick, sumptuous finishes; washes are flatter and have a clean, fresh appearance.

Both the combination and sequence of colours are im-portant. A darker glaze over a light ground coat will add richness and warmth; a lighter tone over a bright colour will give a touch of brilliance. Experimentation will help you to exploit all the possibilities to the full.

In a small flat or house, it is sometimes satisfying to unify all the rooms with one constant colour. In this three-roomed flat, a grey base coat was used in both the bedroom and the sitting room (illustrated overleaf, centre). The variation is provided by the glazes: in the bedroom, coats in paler greys were loosely applied to give a mottled surface, then stippled with a dry brush (see pages 44-7); in the sitting room, the glazes included some yellow. The effect of the paint finish is to dissolve both the awkward architectural features and the position of the wall itself: an illusion of space is created, yet the rooms are very small. In the bedroom, the lack of colour on the walls focusses attention on the African treasures, and leaves the curtains and bedspread to provide all the warmth that is needed.

USING BROKEN COLOUR

This section discusses individual broken colour techniques, starting with the easiest and going on to cover those which demand more expertise. Most of these methods are defined by the tools you use to achieve them – sponging and ragging are obvious examples. But in other cases, the connection is not so clear-cut. Stippling and spattering, for example, can be carried out by a variety of different means. It is here that terminology can become confusing.

The remedy is not to view the different methods in isolation. Although they are treated separately here for the sake of clarity, they are to some extent interchangeable. Each

technique was probably once the result of a happy accident, stumbled upon when someone was trying to achieve a particular texture or effect. While an appreciation of the basic methods and a respect for the properties of paints are essential, to make the most of broken colour you need to retain the same spirit of experiment.

Experimentation doesn't just mean trying out alternative tools, textures and colour schemes, but looking to see whether a combination of methods might be the answer, whether used side by side or all on one surface. Most professional decorators are characteristically vague when asked

Far left: A large expanse of wall in a stairwell can be very unexciting, but this hallway is an excellent solution to the problem. Inside dragged dowel panels, yellow was ragged over white; below the dado rail, a pale base was sponged over with shades of yellow and green, then rag-rolled. The wall contains enough variety to interest the eye, and daylight is reflected into a dark hall.

Centre: A small amount of yellow in the glaze gives just enough warmth to make this sitting room inviting.

Left: The panels in this semi-octagonal bedroom deliberately emphasize the unusual angles. The broken colour effect within the panels is achieved by using oil- and water-based paints together, exploiting the fact that they will not merge. Stippled with a dry brush (pages 44-7), it becomes a gentle background for pictures and prints.

how they arrived at a particular finish. The result is just as likely to be the product of several, related techniques, used with flair and a dash of originality, as the diligent and expert application of one.

It is also vital to consider the context. Broken colour is so simple and satisfying to do that there is a tendency to go overboard and decorate everything in sight. Large busy surfaces like ragged walls should be set off with plain woodwork. On the other hand, certain techniques like sponging when carried over into the decorative trim actually add coherence to a scheme. A versatile effect like spattering can be a good

way of pulling a room together without being overpowering. If the same colours are used on walls, woodwork, fireplaces and even incidental objects like vases, sculptural interest can be retained without sacrificing any tonal harmony. Varying the sequence of the colours prevents the co-ordinated look from becoming too stifling.

Even if you take care and experiment fully beforehand, finishes do sometimes go wrong; but the beauty of paint is that mistakes are cheap and easy to correct. Often another glaze will do the trick. If the worst comes to the worst, you can simply paint over the top and start again.

GLAZES AND WASHES

To accomplish broken colour techniques it is necessary to have a fundamental grasp of the formulation and application of glazes and washes. To avoid confusing terminology, all oil-based paints thinned to transparency will be referred to as 'glazes', all water-based paints thinned to transparency will be referred to as 'washes'. Colour washing (pages 24-7) does present an exception to this rule. Colour washing can be accomplished by using either oil- or water-based paints, hence it is possible to have an oil-based 'wash'.

Types of glaze
A glaze is a semi-transparent film of oil-based colour applied over an opaque ground. There are two main ways of creating a glaze.

Transparent oil glaze is a product available from most paint suppliers, either clear or tinted. It comes in matt, mid-sheen or gloss textures. It can be applied neat but tends to form a skin which prevents the glaze from drying out. It is best thinned in the ratio one part glaze to one part white spirit. The degree of transparency is a measure of its quality. Quality glazes can be very expensive.

Thinned oil paint glaze: White undercoat, flat oil, or eggshell is thinned with white spirit to achieve the required transparency. A thinning ratio of one part paint to three parts white spirit should be satisfactory.

Other possibilities are a home-made glaze formulated by mixing linseed oil and turpentine in the ratio of one to three; and paint glaze. Paint glaze is produced by mixing either undercoat or flat oil paint with transparent oil glaze in the ratio of one to one, then thinning this mixture with an equal quantity of white spirit.

All glazes can be tinted with artist's oil colours, available from paint suppliers or art shops.

Types of wash
A wash is a semi-transparent film of water-based colour applied over an opaque ground. Washes are made by thinning matt or mid-sheen vinyl emulsions with water, in the ratio one part paint to three parts water, depending on the degree of transparency required. As with all glazes and washes, there is no substitute for experimentation.

All washes can be tinted with artist's gouache colours to produce the required tones.

Textural qualities of glazes and washes
Glazes can be prepared in matt, mid-sheen or gloss textures; washes only in matt or mid-sheen. Gloss tends to be rather obvious and revealing, and is often limited to floors and small areas such as furniture or woodwork. It can produce a truly gorgeous effect, such as that of lacquer, and its boldness should be exploited. Where bold patterns are struck, for example in rag-rolling or combing, gloss or mid-sheen finishes can be used to good effect; but the latter should be avoided when attempting fine techniques such as stippling or dragging, where reflection tends to obscure the delicacy of the surface patterning. Matt textures have the widest application and are the safest bet for the novice.

It must be remembered that the texture of the ground coat is as important as the glaze or wash, since it also contributes to the overall surface finish. Matt and mid-sheen textures tend to be the least obtrusive when used as a ground coat. The most satisfactory and successful combination, in fact the choice of the professional, is to use a mid-sheen textured base with a matt textured glaze or wash.

Suitable base coats for glazes and washes
Before you begin, prepare and undercoat your surface, and mask out surrounding areas (see pages 74-7). For the best results you should apply sufficient coats of your base colour to achieve an even colour. Remember that two thin coats are better than one thick one. Provided a surface is clean, dry and free of oil and grease, a glaze can be applied to base coats of matt or mid-sheen emulsion, undercoat, flat oil or eggshell.

A wash can also be applied over matt or mid-sheen emulsion, or, in situations where a subtractive technique is employed and it is necessary to keep the wash alive, over an oil-based ground of undercoat or flat oil paint. The drying time of the wash will be considerably extended.

Sealing the surface

Certain surfaces that may be liable to heavy wear – such as doors, window frames, or walls in kitchens or bathrooms – will need a final protective coat to seal them and make them washable. Polyurethane varnish is a versatile modern product available in matt, mid-sheen or gloss. When thinned it provides an adequate protective layer that can enhance the underlying decorative treatment. One to two coats should be applied, waiting five to six hours between coats.

Varnish will alter the colouring of a decorative finish, making it noticeably yellower. A varnished finish will also respond differently to light, and this could have unfortunate consequences in a room hung with pictures, where areas of wall remain unexposed. You can to some extent avoid these problems by using matt varnish only, or you may prefer not to varnish the walls at all in, for example, bedrooms and sitting rooms, where the surfaces are not subject to particularly heavy wear.

Altering the drying rate

The drying rate of paint may need to be altered if the room is very cold and damp or very hot, or if a subtractive technique is used which demands that the surface remain workable for some time. In general, the thinner the paint the quicker it will dry. Water-based paints dry much faster than oil-based paints – so quickly that they are unsuitable for some subtractive techniques.

The drying rate of oil-based paint can be accelerated by adding liquid dryer (1 teaspoon dryer to ½ litre thinned paint). To slow drying down, add boiled linseed oil (1 teaspoon to ½ litre thinned paint), but bear in mind that this will alter the final colours of your finish, making them yellower, as well as giving the surface a sheen.

In the case of water-based paints, adding a small quantity of glycerine can retard the drying time (1 tablespoon glycerine to 1 litre thinned paint). The drying time of a wash can also be extended by applying it to a mid-sheen textured base coat, especially an oil-based one. Matt textured oil paints, such as undercoat or flat oil paint, will have a similar effect.

Broken colour techniques

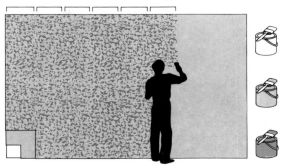

Basic additive technique
Prepare the wall (pages 72-5), and apply undercoat. When dry, apply a white or coloured opaque ground. Allow to dry. Then prepare a glaze or wash and apply in a broken film so that some of the ground is left uncovered. Where the base coat is covered, it will also be subtly modified.

Basic subtractive technique
This method is best done by two people. Prepare and undercoat the surface, and apply the base coat. Working in vertical strips 60 cm (2 ft) wide, one person applies the glaze or wash while the other distresses it, stopping short 15 cm (6 in.) from the leading, wet, edge.

COLOUR WASHING

Colour washing consists of applying an extremely dilute wash or glaze in a continuous film over a ground colour. This is not true broken colour since the surface is not distressed, but successive washes do progressively modify the base coat, giving a depth and brilliance of colour.

Highly effective in both country-style and town house interiors, colour washing creates a soft, pretty background that lifts a room but does not dominate. Because the paint is so dilute, quite strong shades can be used without running the risk of making the room look too dark. It's also a good way to modify a background colour – a thin, red wash or glaze for example, will add a touch of warmth to a yellow base.

You can use water-based washes or oil-based glazes for this technique, and there is a wide variety of effects you can achieve. Either type of paint, depending on its colour and the degree to which it is thinned, can create a room that is luminous and airy, or rich and sophisticated. The main difference is that oil-based paint is more hard-wearing than water-based, and for this technique probably easier to use. For the purist, a wash or glaze consisting almost entirely of diluted artist's oils or gouache gives a particularly transparent effect. A variation on this technique is to create a series of washes by adding artist's colours to the paint used for the base coat. Start with a neutral colour, add artist's colour to tint and thin with solvent, then wash over the wall. Add another colour and repeat the process. The result will be subtly unified and harmonious. As another adaptation of the colour washing effect, you could also re-create the soft-textured look of distemper (see page 26).

Although in all cases the paint is too insubstantial to be suitable for distressing, water-based washes have an inherently distressed finish, since they always display the marks of the tool used to apply them. This random patterning adds to the general impression of rustic charm.

Oil-based colour washes

For colour washing, dilute the paint (flat oil or undercoat) in the ratio 1:8 or 1:9 paint to white spirit. Drying rates will vary according to temperature and humidity, so if the paint

Colour washes need not always be very dilute. Here a white base coat has been washed with just a few coats of vivid yellow, then stencilled. It is a simple way to achieve a brilliant surface.

threatens to be too 'wet', reduce the proportion of white spirit and use the paintbrush itself to move the paint around. If it is impossible to keep a wet edge, decrease the drying rate by adding linseed oil, but remember that this has a yellowing effect on the colour of the glaze.

The application of glazes is a messy business and it is essential to protect against spilling and splashing. It is also advisable to have plenty of clean cloths to hand. These can be used instead of a brush to dab the glaze on to the wall. The glaze must then be brushed out in the direction of natural light. As a rule, thinned paint glaze is messier and more difficult to handle than transparent oil glaze.

The glaze will dry in 24 hours. After this time another coat can be applied, either in the same colour or in a different shade, which can give a rich and lustrous finish.

Water-based colour washes

Dilute matt emulsion in the ratio of 1:9 paint to water. If the day is very hot and the paint is drying too quickly, a small amount of glycerine can be added to slow the drying rate down.

Prepare and paint the surface with your chosen ground colour, and ensure it is clean and grease-free. Avoid drip marks and 'tide lines' by applying the wash with swift, vigorous brush strokes. This will also ensure that you don't linger on one spot too long and begin to dissolve the underlying colour. The wash dries so quickly that brush marks are inevitable, but this fresh, unrefined look can be very pleasing.

After half an hour the wash will be dry and another coat can be applied. It takes at least two coats for the wall really to come to life, and sometimes four or five for the full effect. If you intend to varnish the surface, wait three to four days and then apply two coats of matt clear varnish: this will protect the finish and give a degree of depth.

Pure colour washes

A highly transparent finish can be created by diluting artist's gouache or artist's oils with water or white spirit respectively and applying this over a pale ground. In the case of gouache, a small amount of emulsion should be added to the wash to give it body; in the case of oils, a transparent 'gel' can be added for body.

The colour will richen and deepen with successive applications. Brush the wash on to a dry surface, with quick strokes so that the underlying paint is not removed.

Distemper

Now out of production, distemper was an extremely cheap household paint that could cover a variety of surfaces without too much preparation. Its soft, textured finish made it popular for surfaces that were not perfectly even, or where a quick result was required.

A similar effect today can be achieved by purchasing the ingredients from a trade supplier and mixing them up at home. Although making your own distemper is a protracted business, some people think the effort is worthwhile. (A similar effect can be obtained by applying a wash of flat oil over a trade eggshell base coat.)

Recipe for Distemper

3 kg (1 ⅓ lb) bag whiting, decorator's glue, powder paint

Make the glue according to the manufacturer's instructions, dissolving it in hot water – it should contain alum, a substance which prevents the formation of mould. Leave the glue to cool and set to a jelly. When you are ready to use it, reheat it until it becomes runny.

Half-fill a small bucket with cold water and pour in the whiting until it rises above the surface. Allow to soak for one hour and then stir.

Dissolve the powder colour in cold water and add it a little at a time to the whiting until you like the shade.

Add the warm, runny glue to the dissolved whiting, stirring thoroughly. If it stiffens, reheat gently. This mixture can now be used as a base coat. For a wash, dilute with water to a milky consistency. Distemper will only keep for two days.

Colour washing

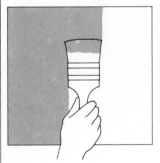 

1. Cover a suitably prepared surface with a base colour and allow to dry overnight. Prepare a very dilute glaze or wash in the required colour.

2. Brush on the glaze or wash, working quite quickly to avoid drips; you can go over it with a dry brush. Apply several coats to achieve a rich, deep finish.

Left: The mirrors in this hallway do much to give an illusion of space, and the paint techniques also play their part well, suggesting the effect of stone. The lower half of the walls are colour washed: each successive wash was created by adding solvent and artists' oils in greys and greens to the original, grey, base colour. Above, grey was ragged on.

Below: Walls the intensity and richness of silk were created here by washing oil-based red glaze over a base coat of pink. The brush strokes are clearly evident, and give depth and texture to the effect. To give a sheen to the surface, a transparent glaze was used as the final coat. It is an extravagantly bold finish, deceptively easy to achieve.

SPONGING

Sponging is the easiest and most adaptable of the true broken colour techniques. It can be either an additive technique – 'sponging on' – or a subtractive one – 'sponging off'. As the term implies, it involves the use of a sponge, either to dab on a broken layer of colour or to distress a wet surface.

Either oil-based or water-based paint can be used. Emulsion will give a soft effect; oil is crisper and cleaner. Texture and transparency can be varied too; the sponge wash or glaze can be shiny or matt, opaque or translucent, depending on the type of paint and the degree of dilution.

All of these variables add up to a highly versatile finish. Sponging can range from the subtle and sophisticated to the outrageously obvious; sponging off gives the softest effect. The coherence of sponging techniques means that they are useful for camouflaging unsightly features such as radiators and pipes or for softening unfortunate proportions. But they can also be used in a purely decorative way on vases, cabinets and tables – in fact on any suitably prepared surface.

Experiment with different colour combinations before you begin. Lining paper provides a cheap medium for investigating colours and textures and for practising sponging techniques. Just two colours can be very effective; more than three can become confused and muddy without careful handling. Where more than two colours are used, the lighter shades should be applied last and the darker ones used sparingly.

Which colours you use will depend on your decorative scheme but, in general, the closer the colours are in tone and in shade, the more subtle and sophisticated the effect will be. But don't be afraid to try something more daring. A dilute glaze or wash of a bright colour over white can look very fresh without being brash; for a bolder look, try mixing primaries or accenting two closer shades with a complementary colour.

Sponging on

Apply two coats of the base colour on top of a suitably prepared surface. Allow to dry overnight.

Prepare the sponge by wetting it with water and wringing it out thoroughly. Place the glaze in a sloping tray and dip the

Left: Sponging on can be a very positive treatment, as this example shows. The technique makes good camouflage for pipes and electrical sockets, and for imperfections in the plaster.

Top: A jardiniere is stencilled over an evenly sponged wall to make a focus for a turn in the stairs. The sponging was in two coats over white emulsion, the second lighter than the first.

Below: Paint effects can exist harmoniously alongside wallpaper. Here a radiator has been camouflaged by sponging on three different colours to match the speckled paper.

sponge into it, removing the excess on the side of the tray. Dab the sponge on to paper until you achieve the right sort of print. The sponge should be almost dry so that the print shows a distinct texture. If the sponge is too wet, the texture will be blurry and the paint will tend to run down the wall.

Work quickly and systematically over the surface, trying for a consistent density. Wring the sponge out from time to time to prevent a build-up of colour obscuring the texture. If you are going to apply two glazes or washes, allow more of the ground colour to show through when applying the first coat. Leave the first glaze or wash to dry overnight before applying the second.

Sponging off

In the same way as for sponging on, a coloured ground is prepared and allowed to dry, then a coloured glaze is applied all over the surface. While it is still wet and workable, the surface is distressed with a wet or dry sponge to remove patches of glaze.

The main problem with this technique is the drying time of the glaze or wash. If you use water-based paints, you will need a friend to help you – it's often a race against time, with one person applying the wash and the other distressing the surface. The drying time can be slowed down by adding linseed oil to oil-based paint or glycerine to water-based paint. If the ground coat is mid-sheen, the glaze or wash is also easier to sponge off. Using water-based paint over an oil-based undercoat will also extend the drying time and enable a more consistent pattern to be achieved.

Work in vertical strips about 60 cm (2 feet) wide, distressing all but 15 cm (6 in.) of the leading edge so that the next section can be blended in without losing continuity of pattern. While one person is distressing, the next strip of glaze can be applied by the other. If you get a build-up of colour on the sponge, wait until you reach a corner before washing it out in solvent, and then brush a little paint on to the sponge before starting again: you want to avoid getting a new 'print' in the middle of a wall.

Sponging on

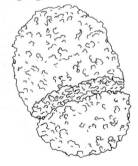

It is preferable to use a marine or 'natural' sponge rather than a synthetic one. Cut off a section, or use all the sponge: choose an interesting plane.

1. Cover a suitably prepared surface with two coats of base colour. Allow to dry overnight. Prepare the glaze or wash by tinting and diluting.

2. Soak sponge in water and wring dry. Dip it into paint, testing print on paper. Sponge quickly and evenly, and clean the sponge only at a corner.

3. For more than one colour, make the first application fairly sparse. Overlap the second glaze or wash. Use a different sponge for each colour.

Used creatively, colour contributes immeasurably to the richness of a sponged surface. Here shades of yellow and a little blue have been sponged over a pale base coat, and below the rail yellow, white and blue have been sponged on in successive layers. The sponged-on blue is very fine indeed, but still manages to pick up the blue of the woodwork and unify the entire wall.

Sponging off

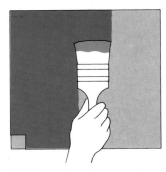

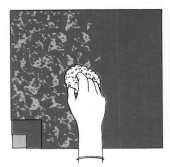

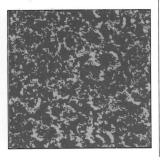

1. Cover a prepared surface with two coats of base colour. Since this technique involves working a wet glaze or wash, enlist a friend's help.

2. Prepare the glaze or wash. One person applies this in a continuous film with a brush, working in strips about 60 cm (2 ft) wide.

3. While the glaze is still wet, the other person distresses it with a sponge, working up to 15 cm (6 in.) of the leading, wet, edge.

4. Wring out sponge regularly to prevent build-up of paint on the sponge. Use a different sponge for each colour to avoid mixing shades.

RAGGING

Ragging is the general term for a whole family of techniques in which a rag or cloth is used to distress the surface. 'Ragging on' is an additive method where the colour is dabbed on; 'ragging off' is a subtractive method where the colour is dabbed off. The texture of the cloth and the type of dabbing action together produce a distinctive pattern.

The most dramatic type of ragging, however, is a version known as 'rag-rolling'. Here a bunched rag is rolled down over the surface, either adding or lifting off patches of glaze to create a dense texture remarkably similar in appearance to crushed velvet. Whereas the other ragging methods are quite static in effect, rag-rolling displays not so much the texture of the cloth as a sense of movement.

Ragging is a good way of camouflaging unsightly pipes or radiators or covering up imperfections in a surface. The technique is also versatile enough for decorating on a much smaller scale, for accentuating furniture, woodwork, vases and fireplaces. It is not a good idea, however, to rag everything in sight – the effect can easily become overpowering, so err on the side of restraint. Ragging on is probably the best way of decorating objects. Since the physical action of rolling demands a flat expanse, rag-rolling is unsuitable for surfaces with tight contours.

Choice of cloth adds greatly to the scope of these techniques. There are no hard and fast rules, but in general the crisper the fabric, the more defined the pattern. For a subtle, more evocative look, use a soft cloth with a close weave. Hessian, chamois, net, dishcloths and even vests all produce interesting textures – experiment with a range of rags to identify the effect you're seeking. When using the rag to remove the glaze or wash, the texture will also vary according to whether the cloth is used dry or wetted with water. Dry cloths produce a clearer pattern.

Whichever cloth you use, however, the overall effect can easily become oppressive if colours are not restrained. It's best to play safe and opt for pastel or neutral shades, fairly close in tone, especially if you're ragging a large area. Even off-white ragged over a white ground can be striking, for the patterning is itself emphatic enough.

Far left: Ragging can produce a very uniform effect, which many find overpowering on a large area. One answer is to apply the glaze in patches, as in this hallway. Blue has been ragged over white, but not consistently over the entire surface. The result successfully avoids monotony.

Left: Another answer to the same problem is to contain ragging within panels (see also page 20). Here the front room of a town house has been transformed into a sophisticated, elegant drawing room by painting the walls with trompe l'oeil panelling, achieved with the dragging technique (pages 36-9). Inside the panels a yellow glaze has been ragged off with a very wet rag, which produces this soft, rather diffused effect.

Using the cloth

For ragging on or off, a rhythmic, systematic dabbing action is used to achieve uniform coverage. To prevent the finish from becoming mechanical and repetitive, adjust the cloth regularly and vary the wrist action.

For rag-rolling, it is crucial to vary the rolling action to prevent the surface becoming too insistent. Rearrange the cloth, apply different amounts of pressure and change the rolling direction.

Cloths should be abandoned once they have become sodden with glaze, so ensure you have a plentiful supply before you begin. It is not advisable to change the texture of the cloth half-way through. All cloths should be clean, lint-free and dye-fixed. It is essential to dispose of used rags carefully because of the fire hazard.

Types of paint

Ragging can be successfully achieved using either oil- or water-based paints, depending on the look you want to obtain. For subtractive techniques, oil-based paints are preferable since the surface will remain workable for longer. Rolling off, however, is relatively quick to do so the drying time is less critical.

The drying time of water-based paints can be extended by adding a small amount of glycerine to the paint, by not thinning the paint or by applying it over a silk or mid-sheen base coat.

Another method is, contrary to normal procedure, to apply water-based paint over an oil-based ground – undercoat or flat oil, for example. This base coat must be clean, dry and degreased. Experiment to arrive at the right consistency for the top coat – if it is too thin it will run off.

Ragging or rolling on

Over a prepared surface, apply a base coat in the required shade with a roller or brush. Thin the glaze or wash to the required consistency.

Dip the cloth in the tray, removing the excess on the side, and test on paper until you get the print you want. For ragging

Ragging on

 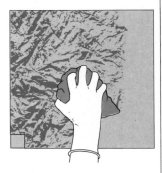

1. Paint on a base coat. Thin glaze or wash to required consistency. Dip cloth in paint and test print on paper.

2. Dab on paint with bunched cloth. Vary the action and adjust cloth, and change to a clean cloth regularly.

Ragging off

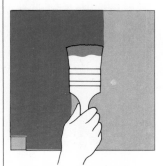 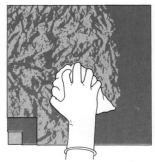

1. Paint on base coat and allow to dry overnight. One person then applies the glaze or wash, working in vertical strips about 60cm (2ft) wide.

2. While the paint is still wet, the other person distresses it with a wet or dry cloth, stopping short 15 cm (6 in.) from the edge.

Rag-rolling on

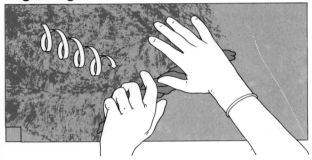

1. Apply base coat. Prepare glaze or wash. Roll cloth into a sausage shape and soak in glaze or wash.

2. Roll the cloth down over the surface. To avoid a mechanical texture, change direction and adjust cloth.

Rag-rolling off

1. Apply a base coat and allow to dry overnight. Then one person applies a glaze or wash with a brush, working in vertical strips.

2. While the paint is still wet, the other person rolls the cloth down over the surface to lift off patches of paint. Avoid a mechanical texture.

on, dab the cloth systematically over the surface, adjusting the motion and rebunching the cloth regularly to avoid repetitive patterning. For rag-rolling, roll the cloth up loosely in a sausage shape and roll over the surface slowly and steadily to prevent smudging. Vary the direction and pressure. Change cloths regularly.

Ragging or rolling off

Prepare the ground coat, and apply the glaze or wash in a single film in vertical strips 60 cm (2 feet) wide. Use the cloth, either dry or dipped in solvent if you want a softer effect, to distress the surface, stopping short 15 cm (6 in.) from the leading edge. This margin is distressed when the next strip of top coat is applied. Change cloths regularly.

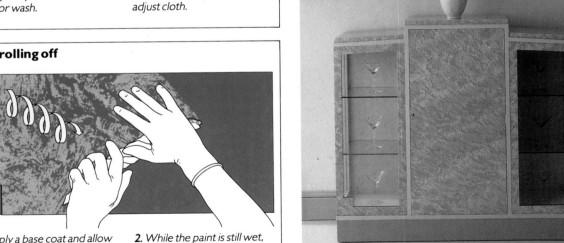

Exploit the emphatic qualities of rag-rolling to create a rhythmic signature. This sideboard has white rolled over a blue ground: *the vase has blue ragged on to white. In the background the wall is sponged, blue over white, and the skirting dragged.*

DRAGGING AND COMBING

Dragging

An elegant, formal treatment, dragging is a subtractive distressing technique in which a fine dry brush is gently dragged through a thin wet glaze to produce a series of parallel lines where the ground colour is exposed. On walls it makes a refined backdrop for a sophisticated interior. It's best, too, on smooth surfaces, since the dragged effect will only exaggerate any imperfections. For this reason, while dragging will enhance a sound, well-proportioned room, it is not a good way to disguise irregularities.

Traditionally, dragging is carried out vertically, making an even texture reminiscent of woven fabric. But by using more than one glaze and distressing horizontally or diagonally, as well as vertically, a whole range of different effects can be created, from an open-weave homespun look to something more akin to shot silk.

Apart from walls, any flat surface can be dragged if it is suitably prepared. Dragging is particularly effective on woodwork, doors and furniture, provided the strokes run in the direction of the wood grain. This is a good way of adding colour without sacrificing the impression of graininess.

A well-established professional technique, dragging does

Far left: Glazes for dragging are usually assumed to be of one colour, but this treatment opens up new possibilities. Over a creamy-yellow background massive zigzag stripes were loosely painted all around the walls, using white paint diluted with solvent and coloured brown, rust and orange with artists' oils. The walls were then dragged, and this subtle, almost Italianate effect was the result.

Left and below: Classical dragging at its best. The pink glaze is peculiarly perfect for this elegant paint effect.

require a degree of expertise. To achieve success you need a steady hand – practising first on small areas like cupboard doors and tables may help. You must also be prepared to spend money on a quality dragging brush – the bristles are flexible enough to avoid a mechanical pinstriped effect. If you can't afford the outlay, wallpaper brushes or jamb brushes make acceptable compromises, although the finish will lack a degree of definition. Dragging, like all subtractive techniques, can be made much easier by enlisting the help of a friend. One person applies the glaze or wash while the other distresses it before it becomes unworkable.

Using oil-based paint

Prepare the surface and apply a base coat in the required colour. Mix the glaze to the right consistency and apply it in vertical strips 60 cm (2 feet) wide, with a 10 cm (4 in.) brush.

Using a dragging brush (or suitable substitute), distress the glaze by dragging through the paint in continuous vertical strokes. As a guide, you can draw vertical lines in blue chalk on the ground coat or suspend a plumb-line from a picture rail. Stop short 15 cm (6 in.) from the leading edge of the glaze, distressing this strip when the next application of glaze has been made.

Using water-based paint

As with all subtractive techniques, washes of emulsion dry too quickly for a consistent finish. The drying time can be slowed by applying the wash over a vinyl silk ground, which will also dry to a slight sheen. The ground could also be flat oil or undercoat, provided it is clean, dry and degreased. A small amount of glycerine added to water-based paint will also retard drying. Do not over-thin the wash or it will run off the surface. The help of a second person makes the distressing of water-based washes considerably easier.

Combing

Combing, a close relative of dragging, is a bold, versatile, subtractive technique that offers considerable scope in its application. The striking patterns you can achieve are particularly suited to decorating floors, where the subtleties of a dragged finish would be lost underfoot.

The characteristics of this finish are a direct function of the distressing tool, the comb. Although you can buy combs in a variety of sizes and materials from paint suppliers or decorators' shops, this is an unnecessary expenditure. Creating a pattern that bears the signature of a comb you have made can be very satisfying.

Tools and techniques

If the room is very high, stop at waist height and then drag upwards from the floor. Stagger the place where you stop and feather the joins. Dragging upwards for 30 cm (12 in.) at the bottom of each strip will prevent a build-up of glaze near the skirting board.

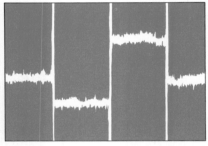

Dragging

Dragging is most easily carried out by two people. Apply a base coat and allow to dry (1). One person paints on a glaze or wash in vertical strips 60 cm (2 ft) wide (2). While this is still wet, the other person distresses the surface by drawing a dry dragging brush down through the paint, stopping short 15 cm (6 in.) from the leading, wet, edge.

I

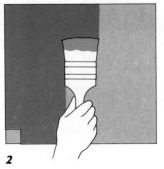

2

3

These kitchen units had a red glaze applied over an off-white base colour, which was then freely distressed with a bought graining comb. The combing technique reveals a lot of the base coat, and in the process a great deal of glaze is displaced: wrapping a rag around the comb will soak up some of this excess, and prevent large deposits of paint at the edges.

The size of the teeth will give the scale of the pattern. The larger the pattern, the bolder the colours can be. In such cases, you will also need to reduce the transparency of the glaze or wash, leaving it more opaque. Combing can never achieve the lightness and refinement of a dragged finish, so it is often better to exploit its directness and forcefulness. Varying the pattern by using different combs can add interest.

Types of paint

With a few exceptions, the combing technique is the same as that of dragging. Most importantly, the undercoat must be substantial enough to withstand abrasion by the comb.

For oil-based paint, the base undercoat should be trade eggshell, which will dry with a slight sheen. For emulsion, use vinyl silk, which also has a sheen finish. These harder surfaces withstand distressing better and allow paint to be more easily moved around on top. When using oil-based paint, there is the added advantage that the top coat will not dry out so quickly, prolonging the distressing time. Apply the glaze in sections that can be easily worked while the glaze is wet.

Protective coats of polyurethane varnish should then be applied. This is very important where the surface will be subject to heavy wear, such as a floor, or walls in kitchens.

Combs

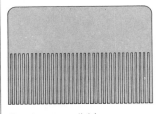

Combs are available commercially from decorators' shops (above) but it is easy and satisfying to make your own (right). Use semi-rigid materials like rubber, hardboard or perspex; experiment by cutting teeth at different intervals and thicknesses.

Combing

Apply a base coat over a suitably prepared surface. When this is dry, apply a glaze or wash, thinned to the required consistency, adjusting the drying time if necessary. While this is still wet, draw the comb down over the surface to create the pattern. If the surface will be exposed to heavy wear, protective coats of polyurethane varnish should then be applied.

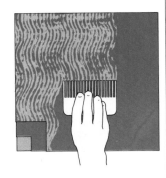

SPATTERING AND CISSING

Spattering

Spattering is a simple additive technique which consists of showering flecks of paint over a uniformly coloured ground. Since there is no one tool to define the method and no formal rules governing the size, colour, density or position of the paint flecks, the scope is vast. The effect can range from a fine misting of colour to a more cavalier treatment where blobs of paint are flung at a surface. It's versatile, too – spattering can be applied to almost any surface, from walls to lamp bases, mirror frames or fireplaces.

The limiting factor is your imagination. Experiment with a range of different techniques and colours on lining paper or a sheet of hardboard. Primary colours over a white ground will give a gay, light-hearted look; subtle differences of tone, such as mauve over grey, are more sophisticated. Where several colours are used, you can set off a couple of close shades like cream and light brown with a sparse application of black. Colour is not the only consideration: contrasting the texture of the paints – for example, spattering matt paint over a mid-sheen or gloss ground – gives you another range of interesting options.

Because this is an additive technique, oil- and water-based paints are equally effective, although the speed at which emulsions dry gives them an advantage when multiple overlaps of colour are required.

Spattering with a brush

Virtually any stiff-bristled brush mounted on a shaft is suitable. A large stencilling brush, with its squared end, is most effective for large surfaces; for detailed work a toothbrush is hard to beat. Release the paint flecks by running your finger over the bristles or by striking the shaft of the brush on a straight edge. Running the brush over fine chicken wire will also given the same effect.

The density and size of the flecks is a function of the paint dilution, the distance from the surface and the force applied to the bristles or shaft of the brush, and prior experimentation is important. This is a messy technique, so take adequate precautions against spilling and splashing.

Safety precautions
To avoid inhaling the spray when spattering with paint atomizers or spray guns, it is essential to wear a mask and goggles. It is also a good idea to keep a window open to allow fumes to escape.

Right: Spattering techniques have been used in this room with great delicacy, so much so that it almost has the stamp of more subtle broken colour effects like sponging. A cheap spray gun was used to spatter pink, cream, grey and a little raspberry paint over a base of blue-grey. The result makes the room quietly inviting and harmonious, and successfully avoids the busy effect that spattering can sometimes produce.

Below: Here blue paint has been spattered very regularly over white, producing a homogeneous effect that is the hallmark of the technique.

Spattering with a spray

For a fine, misted effect, spattering can be carried out using a paint atomizer, a simple instrument available from any model-making shop. A cheap alternative is an ordinary perfume spray. The scale of the tool and delicacy of the spatter means that application is limited to furniture or to picking out fine detail.

For work on a larger scale, you could hire an electric spray gun. Experiment with different nozzles, pressures and paint densities to get the effect you want. It is essential to wear goggles and a mask to avoid inhaling the spray.

Cissing

A variation of spattering is a distressing technique known as cissing. The bristles of a spattering brush are dipped in neat solvent – either water or white spirit, depending on which type of paint is used – and the solvent is then flicked on to a surface glaze or wash. The glaze or wash, which should still be wet and workable, will actually open up, forming pools of diluted colour. The effect can vary from a light, regularly

Using a spray

Paint atomizers, available from model-making shops, produce a misted effect. Even cheap ones give a good effect. Perfume sprays are an alternative.

Stencil brush

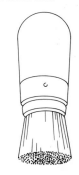

The best tool for spattering and cissing is the square-ended stencil brush, although any stiff-bristled brush with a squared end will do the job efficiently.

Spattering

I. Apply a base coat to a suitably prepared surface and allow to dry. Mix up a glaze or wash and experiment with different dilutions to get the effect you want. Dip the squared end of a stencil brush, or similar, into the paint. Release flecks by striking the shaft on a straight edge.

2. An alternative method is to run your thumb over the end of the stencil brush to release the paint. Vary the distance between brush and surface.

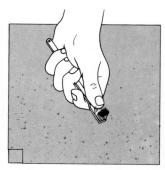

3. For really fine results, dip a toothbrush into the paint and draw your thumb over the bristles to release tiny flecks of glaze or wash.

patterned texture reminiscent of porphyry to the random cloudiness often exhibited by marble. With oil-based paint, methylated spirit can be used as an alternative to solvent to create larger 'pools'; an atomizer will provide greater control.

Cissing should always be carried out on horizontal surfaces, otherwise the diluted paint will drip. A clean dry cloth or sponge can be used to control the effect and mop up any excess solvent, and you could also use it to brush out and soften the pools to make an even more blurred finish. Goggles are again recommended protective equipment.

You can achieve a similar effect to cissing without going to the trouble of painting on a base coat and a glaze: there is a proprietary brand of paint called Hammerite which will do the work for you. This is a metallic paint available in a range of colours which, when brushed over a surface, forms itself into a tight, uniform pattern and creates an effect very similar to that of regular cissing (follow the manufacturer's instructions). Used with sensitivity and imagination this can be truly stunning, but as always experiment with it first in case it is too bold for the surface you had in mind.

Spattering just the details in a room can be supremely effective, for the technique often looks its best when carried out with restraint. Mask out surrounding areas with tape and newspaper, and take care not to flick paint outside your chosen area. Here a beam draws the eye towards a mezzanine study, and the heavy black gloss paint on the ladder and balustrade makes an excellent contrast to the fine, understated spattering.

Cissing

Paint on a base coat and allow to dry. Then apply a glaze or wash. While this is still wet, spatter with the appropriate solvent – either water or white spirit. Cissing is easiest on horizontal surfaces: control the effect by mopping up excess dribbles of glaze with a dry cloth.

STIPPLING AND SHADING

Stippling

A fine, freckled finish is the hallmark of stippling, a subtractive technique used extensively throughout the whole range of decorative painting. Its delicacy makes it ideal for a restrained backdrop but its application is often remedial since it provides a good way of disguising brush strokes, or of softly blending colours. Applying a stippled glaze can also rescue an unsuccessful finish.

When stippling, a glaze is applied to a coloured ground and, while it is still workable, a flat-faced brush is used to strike the surface quickly and rhythmically. This action lifts off flecks of glaze, exposing the underlying colour. Where the glaze remains, the ground colour is modified.

Traditionally, a darker coloured glaze or wash is applied over a lighter background. This has the effect of intensifying the original colour, particularly if the shades are close together. A stippled glaze can also substantially alter the tone of the background – warming up a cool colour or *vice versa*. If the shades are further apart the effect will be less predictable, so prior experimentation is, as always, a good idea.

There are some drawbacks. Over large surfaces, stippling can be monotonous and exhausting to do, demanding a good deal of concentration to achieve a uniform density. And, as with all subtractive techniques, there is a problem with the faster-drying water-based paints. Enlisting the aid of a friend can help overcome both these problems, but the same person should do all the stippling so that the pattern remains uniform. The drying time can also be extended by using mid-sheen paints, and by adding small amounts of glycerine.

Professional stippling brushes are very expensive and not indispensable, so it is worth investigating alternatives. Virtually any flat-faced brush will do; each will leave its own distinctive mark. Possibilities include a decorator's dusting brush, stove brush, grooming brush, rubber-tipped stippling brush and even a broom with squared-off bristles. A broom can be handy for stippling ceilings.

You can speed up the process to some extent by using rollers. Lambswool or mohair varieties are the best; synthetic ones tend to skid and smudge the glaze. Several cheap scrubbing brushes nailed to a flat board can also enable you to stipple a large, flat area more quickly. Whatever type of brush you use, clean it regularly to prevent more glaze or wash being deposited than is removed.

Shading

Shading consists of blending colours from light to dark across a surface to simulate the effect of natural light. This creates a spatial illusion – walls can be drawn in or spaced out, ceilings can be made to seem higher or lower than they really are. An essential element in the effect is a gradual transition from one shade to the next, and this is achieved by painting the shades in bands, separated by strips of the ground colour. Each painted band is then stippled, so that flecks of paint are lifted on to the brush and transferred to the adjoining strips of base coat. The result is a completely stippled wall that fades gradually from one colour to the next, an effect that relies for its success on the ability of the stippling technique to 'dissolve' colours and give them depth.

You can use more than one colour in the transition from light to dark, or dark to light, but they should all be pastel shades and be similar in tone. For an average-sized room three shades will be sufficient; a larger room may require five. Opaque colours can be used, but a transparent glaze will give a much more ethereal quality. Shading is extremely difficult with water-based paint, since it dries so quickly that the bands are almost impossible to stipple effectively. Oil-based paint is preferable since it dries more slowly.

Before you begin, draw guidelines on the surface to indicate where the bands are to start and end, using pale blue chalk that will disappear when the paint is applied. The lines can be horizontal or vertical, depending on the effect required; for a ceiling a centre must be established and concentric circles drawn around this point.

Right: In this room the plasterwork cornice had been removed in the 1930s; rather than put it back, the owners decided to exploit the gently curving corners and shade the room from yellow to white. Stippling makes this possible.

Stippling

Although professional stippling brushes are designed specifically for the job, they are very expensive. Luckily, cheaper alternatives will do just as well. Any flat-faced brush can be used, including a dusting brush, stove brush, grooming brush or even a broom with squared-off bristles. Brooms can be very useful for stippling inaccessible places such as ceilings. Nail several scrubbing brushes to a flat board to stipple a large area quickly, or try using a roller of natural fibre.

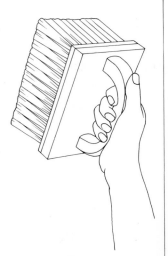

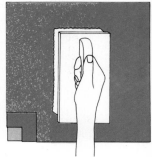

1. Cover a suitably prepared surface with a base coat and allow to dry. Then one person applies a glaze or wash with a brush, working in vertical strips 60 cm (2 ft) wide. Speed is now of the essence.

2. While the glaze or wash is still wet, the other person strikes the surface with a flat-faced brush, lifting off flecks of glaze. One person should do all the stippling to keep the pattern consistent.

The shading in this room creates a double illusion: that of colour fading from dark to light; and that of blue fading to green. In fact the effect was created by gradually adding white to blue, painting and stippling the room in bands. Four tints of blue were used, with the last an off-white. Thus was a tiny room transformed into a restful and luminous space.

Shading

Apply a ground coat of a pale colour. Prepare three glazes or washes, each slightly darker than the last. Apply these in bands from light to dark, leaving bands of the ground colour in between. While the paint is still wet, stipple across the painted bands so that flecks of paint are transferred to the base coat – you will need as many stippling brushes as glazes. This is a job for two people, one to apply the glaze or wash and the other to stipple the bands of shade.

Shading is most usually carried out in horizontal bands, with the aim of creating an effect that will raise or lower a ceiling. However, it can also be applied vertically – working from dark to light and then to dark again, or vice versa. The result will be to change the apparent size and scale of a room in a most dramatic way.

TREATMENTS OF ILLUSION

The techniques discussed over the next few pages take decorative painting a step further, into the realm of illusion. Most of these treatments, increasingly popular in home decorating, involve simulating a natural material such as wood, marble or tortoiseshell. Also included in this section are antiquing, the process of artificially ageing a surface; stencilling, a simple, stylized way of making patterns; and, the height of artistic deception, *trompe l'oeil*.

Broken colour techniques form the basis for many of these effects, but some will also require a degree of artistic expertise. For this reason, it is advisable at least to have the help of a professional practitioner, if not to ask one to execute whatever illusionistic effect you're after. One important difference between illusion and broken colour that an amateur should bear in mind is the scale of application. Illusion is rarely suitable for an expanse of wall and is best kept for furniture, detail and decorative trim – as an accent rather than as wholesale embellishment. This is not only because most of these effects are busy and detailed but also because they refer specifically to a natural material, and that imposes certain constraints. A tortoiseshelled floor or a marbled ceiling is really visual nonsense; but it must also be said that with skill and wit you can overcome such limitations.

Traditionally, painted illusion arose in response to a demand for cost-effective finishes. With the real materials often expensive or hard to obtain, craftsmen were called upon to create authentic reproductions, as indistinguishable from the real thing as possible. Today, while economy remains an important factor, the emphasis is equally on fun and creative expression, opening up the possibility for a freer interpretation of colour and design; there is a more light-hearted approach, that puts illusionistic effects well within the reach of the amateur. Illusion need no longer be viewed as a substitute for the genuine article, but as yet another creative option at the home decorator's disposal.

A wall stripped of wallpaper was the inspiration for this colourful and original effect, and the painters set out to create an illusion of a decaying room recently stripped bare – but without sacrificing vivid colour. The finish has a tarnished, aged effect that was achieved with a panoply of paint techniques, including marbling and dragging, and the result gives a richly luminous effect to the kitchen in which it appears.

ANTIQUING

When a surface ages naturally, it acquires a mellow, lived-in look that is both reassuring and easy on the eye. This effect can be simulated by 'antiquing', a process by which surfaces are artificially aged using a number of distressing techniques already described under Broken Colour. The aim is to soften and modify proportions by adding a patina of age. There are different techniques for walls, woodwork and furniture.

Walls

Freshly painted walls are often brash and uncompromising in appearance. Particularly in a period interior, redecoration can look too crisp, making an unfortunate contrast with furnishings that have mellowed with time. The remedy is to cover the walls with a tinted wash or glaze, which has the effect of enriching and deepening the ground colour.

The choice of tinter is important. Generally, small amounts of raw or burnt umber will create a warm tone without radically changing the colour. The principle is the same as for colour washing (see pages 24-7). Either oil- or water-based paint can be used, applying as many glazes or washes as necessary to achieve the required colour. Remember that if water-based paint is used, the brush strokes will be visible because of the quick drying time, but this can be effective in a country-style setting. Protect the finished surface if necessary with one coat of polyurethane varnish.

Woodwork

When wood ages, if unprotected by paint or varnish, it tends to lighten, with the grain showing up in contrast. To simulate this, prepare any natural wood surface by making sure it is clean, dry and degreased. Then make a wash or glaze that is lighter than the natural colour of the wood and apply it with a brush. Immediately wipe off the excess with a clean cloth. The remainder of the paint will soak in. When the surface is dry, sand it down to highlight the grain.

Furniture

Wooden furniture that has been cared for over a long period of time exhibits certain characteristics. It tends to have a dull lustre created by successive layers of polish, with dark areas in inaccessible places and light areas where heavy use or polishing has occurred. Antiquing furniture is essentially a process of reproducing this shading using tinters such as burnt umber, burnt sienna and lamp black to achieve the greens, browns and reds associated with ageing.

First, clean the piece by rubbing it all over with methylated spirit and wire wool to remove wax and grease. Wipe with white spirit and allow to dry. Make a glaze using white eggshell and the required tinters, thinned one part paint to three parts

Left: the walls in this kitchen were 'aged' with a mixture of emulsion, powdered filler and sand, which dried to a sandy colour and texture. The cracks were painted freehand on top.

Below: This shows the process described opposite for ageing wood: a glaze is washed over and then rubbed down. The panels at the back have been ragged to look 'degraded'.

white spirit. The glaze should be a couple of tones darker than the natural colour of the piece.

Apply the glaze with a soft brush. When it is just tacky, remove patches of glaze from areas where the most wear might have taken place, by rubbing with a pad of fine wire wool. Blend in light and dark areas, taking care not to disrupt any gilding. You can also use a stencilling brush to spatter fine flecks of brown or black ink on to the surface, which will make the antiquing look even more authentic. Protect the surface with polyurethane varnish.

WOODGRAINING

The natural beauty of wood and the decorative potential of its polished surface have been appreciated throughout history. A vast number of different species have been used in the home for furniture or woodwork, ranging from the familiar oak, ash, walnut and pine to the more exotic teak and ebony. Each has its own distinct character, expressed in terms of colour, texture and pattern of grain.

Popular woodgraining consists of a stylized simulation rather than an accurate replica of the real material. It involves distilling the natural components down to three main features: knots, grain and heartwood. And although a wide variety of colours exist in nature, with woodgraining the range can be extended even further, well beyond the traditional warm shades of yellow, brown and red. The most successful combination, however, is usually tone on tone, with the grain being depicted in the darker colour.

Woodgraining is essentially an extension of the distressing techniques dragging and combing, in which paint is broken up in a series of parallel lines (see pages 36-9); combing originally developed as a graining technique, and the combs were modified to simulate different woods. Woodgraining can be achieved using either oil- or water-based paints. Before you begin, practise constructing graining patterns by tying a row of pencils or coloured crayons to a rule and drawing this along a sheet of lining paper.

Because the patterning is fairly gentle, the application of this technique is a little broader than that of the other illusionist methods. It can be used wherever the appearance of wood is desired, but it can also be a good way of decorating wooden surfaces that are already painted, adding colour while restoring an impression of graininess. Picture frames, door panels and pieces of furniture are all suitable.

Using oil-based paints

Apply a light-coloured eggshell base – cream is often an appropriate colour – over a surface that has already been undercoated. (Natural wood should be primed with a proprietary wood primer before undercoating.) Allow to dry.

Mix a thin glaze (one part paint to one part white spirit) and tint to the predominant colour of the simulated wood. Apply with a brush or cloth. While the surface is still wet, drag the surface with a 75 mm (3 in.) flat brush, fidgeting the parallel lines slightly. Use a dusting brush to soften the lines.

Once this coat is dry, draw in the grain pattern with chalk, remembering to include examples of knots and heartwood as well as grain. Reference to a real piece of wood will help you to be convincing. Using white spirit and artist's oils, mix a deeper shade of the same colour as the glaze. Thin to a workable consistency and draw in the pattern using an artist's brush. The lines can be softened and slightly extended by lightly brushing in the direction of the grain with a clean dusting brush.

Allow to dry and seal with three coats of polyurethane varnish, thinned three parts varnish to one part white spirit.

Using water-based paints

A quick result can be achieved by painting with 'beer'. Thin one bottle of stale brown beer or brown ale with water (one part beer to two parts water). Add sugar (2 teaspoons to 1 pint of thinned beer) and a few drops of detergent. This mixture makes a very translucent graining coat, coloured in shades of deep amber to pale gold. The beer can also be tinted with acrylic or gouache tinters.

The surface must be suitably prepared and undercoated and then painted with a base coat of flat oil, tinted to a suitably neutral colour. When dry, lightly sand this down. Construct guidelines with chalk to establish the pattern and then paint on the grain pattern, using an artist's brush to apply the 'beer'. The finished surface must be protected with two coats of polyurethane varnish.

The great advantage of this method is the quick drying time: 15 minutes. If you are dissatisfied with the result, the paint can be washed off the surface even after it has dried.

Alternatively, the ground can be covered with the mixture and distressed with a comb to make the graining (see page 39). You can use ordinary water-based paints and home-made combs for cheap and cheerful results. Experiment with different combs to establish the sort of markings you want.

Once you have mastered the basic technique of woodgraining there is no reason why you shouldn't attempt it on a larger scale – although not many amateurs would feel confident to attempt panels as large as these. This is a good illustration not just of the technique, but also of the way you can use lighting to show your illusionistic effects off to their best advantage.

Woodgraining

1. Over a suitably prepared surface, paint on a light-coloured base coat using a standard paintbrush. Allow to dry overnight.

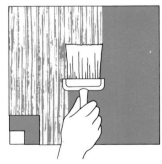

2. Apply a glaze, wash or 'beer' mixture. While still wet, distress by dragging or combing vertically with an appropriate tool (pages 38-9).

3. Use a dusting brush to soften the parallel lines by brushing very gently at right angles to the pattern while the glaze is still wet.

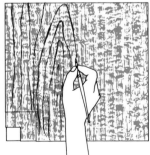

4. Mix a deeper shade of glaze. Paint on grain pattern with an artist's brush. Use crumpled blotting paper for knots. Copy a real piece of wood.

MARBLING

Marble has always presented a challenge to the craftsman. The cool, serene beauty of this natural stone has long been appreciated, but the high cost and difficulty of transporting and handling the material means that there has always been a demand for decorative simulation.

Marble was originally formed when rivers of molten limestone cooled and solidified under great pressure, a process which gives the stone its stratified crystalline structure. Simulating marble involves suggesting its essential characteristics of translucency, depth, cloudiness and motion, using a combination of broken colour techniques, including ragging, sponging, stippling, cissing and spattering.

Inspiration for colour and pattern should be drawn from the tremendous range of shades and textures offered by the natural material. Examining marble fireplaces, tiles and floors will give you some idea of this variety and also suggest ways of applying the technique. Since marble is such a heavy, dense stone, it is particularly suitable for flooring, work surfaces and tiling; avoid applying the technique to such surfaces as ceilings where the real material would never be used.

Using oil-based paint

Achieving translucency and depth: Apply a white or pale base coat of eggshell. Mix up a thin glaze with artist's oils, tinted to a slightly darker shade. A dirty white glaze (with very small amounts of raw umber or black added) over a white base coat will give the effect of the popular white marble.

Apply the glaze with a brush or cloth and rag-roll to expose one-half to two-thirds of the ground (pages 32-5). Soften with a damp or dry sponge or cloth. The glaze can also be rolled on, which gives a slightly sharper pattern. Translucency and depth are achieved by distressing several layers of glaze, each tinted to contrast slightly with the ground colour. Pastels over white are particularly effective.

Achieving cloudiness: While the surface glazes are still workable, a cloudy effect can be achieved by cissing the surface with white spirit (see page 43). This is often known as 'fossilized marbling'. The effect involves spattering flecks of

Opposite, above: A bathroom wall is an obvious candidate for a marbled paint finish. This wall has a strong diagonal accent created by the complicated veining patterns. A white background was ragged over patchily with several glazes, and the veins, in black, red, brown and white, loosely follow this pattern.

Opposite below: Use marbling techniques to create visual witticisms like this dado. Matt black eggshell was used for the background, and white and grey for the veins. The result is both stylized and stylish.

Left: These fake marble slabs are deceptively easy to achieve. The background is a yellow glaze washed over a white ground, and the veins and blocks were painted in a single colour over the top. The result far exceeds the time and effort gone into it: all it requires is a little patience and a straight-edging tool.

solvent randomly over the surface to dissolve the paint glaze into pools of colour. When more than one coloured glaze has been used, the colours merge to form extraordinary patterns and colours. Methylated or white spirit can be used; the former further accentuates the effect. You can control the process to some extent by mopping up excess solvent with a clean dry cloth, but do not attempt cissing on vertical surfaces, for the paint will drip.

To achieve the effect of cloudiness on vertical surfaces, dab with a cloth or sponge, either dry or wetted with water and wrung out thoroughly.

Veining: Perhaps the most striking characteristic of marble is veining, a series of jagged lines which describe a course over the surface and always suggest motion. They usually appear within bands of slightly darker marble. To simulate veining, it might help you to back-light a twig: the shadows projected on the wall can be used for the veining pattern. Choose a colour in artist's oils which contrasts with the glazes used in your background marbling and apply over a wet surface freehand, using a fine sable brush. These lines should then be softened by dabbing with a dry cloth or by running a dry brush or a feather across in all directions. Small flecks of paint can be spattered at intersections – gold or silver metallic paint is useful as highlights. Suggest depth by trapping the veins between different coloured glazes. Finish with one or two coats polyurethane varnish, thinned three parts varnish to one part white spirit.

Make sure that you dispose of all cloths soaked in solvent or glaze very carefully to avoid creating a fire hazard.

Using water-based paint

First apply a matt white base coat in emulsion. Then rag-roll a pastel wash of mid-sheen emulsion over the top. For the veining, use the base colour or a contrasting shade in matt emulsion; metallic paint can also give a dramatic effect. Paint in the veins freehand, using an artist's brush, as above. Smudge or soften these with a cloth and spatter the intersections with a contrasting colour. Repeat the veining process in another colour, following a different path. Protect with polyurethane varnish as for oil-based paint.

Porphyry

Porphyry is a granite-like rock whose surface can be simulated using spattering techniques (pages 40-3) with oil- or water-based paints. Commonly used on fire surrounds and table tops, the predominant colour is red, although green, violet grey and brown types exist. The rock often contains flecks of fool's gold and exhibits a characteristic known as clouding. Simulated porphyry need not slavishly follow nature: unlikely colour combinations can be very pleasing, so don't feel constrained by that suggested here.

The effect of porphyry is very simple to achieve. Sponge a terracotta colour on to a base coat of beige. Then spatter over the entire surface with ivory and black paint, speckling it uniformly but quite sparsely. It can be effective to spatter in metallic paint, although this should be handled carefully as the effect is powerful and can easily detract from the authenticity of the finish. Cissing with water or white spirit (depending on type of paint used) can be undertaken on horizontal surfaces to enhance the effect.

Finish with a varnish when dry, if required.

Marbling is one technique that benefits by a little creative interpretation. This example uses soft browns and neutrals, which find an echo in the pale pink of the walls above the rail. For the marble, three layers of paint were each rag-rolled off and then softened with a dry brush; white 'veins' were then applied. The result is a long way from the chilly feel of real marble, and makes welcoming a dark hallway.

Marbling

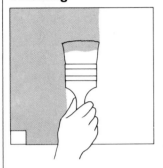

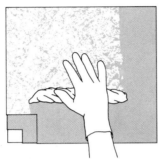

1. Apply a white or pale base coat. Then mix a slightly darker glaze or wash and paint this over the surface using a standard brush.

2. While the glaze or wash is still wet, rag-roll off to expose one-half to two-thirds of the base colour. For a sharper pattern, roll the glaze on.

3. To achieve the characteristic translucency and depth of marble, repeat the process using successive layers of glaze until you are satisfied.

4. Each glaze should be tinted to contrast slightly with the ground colour and with the other glazes, and rag-rolled off – or on – each time.

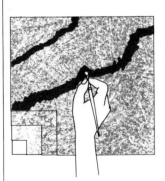

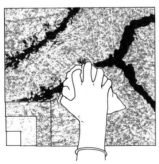

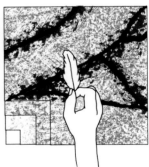

5. Using an artist's brush and a darker glaze or wash, paint on irregular patches about 5 cm (2 in) wide, to suggest areas of compression.

6. While the patches are still wet, rag-roll off to smudge them and preserve the appearance of translucency. Soften with a dry brush.

7. Using a contrasting colour and an artist's brush, paint in the veins freehand, siting them in the darker patches and making them intersect.

8. Soften the veins with a dry brush or feather while still wet. Alternatively, the veins can be painted in with a goose or pheasant's feather.

TORTOISESHELLING

A tortoiseshelled surface is rich and sophisticated. Characterized by a striking pattern, this treatment is best used in a setting that complements rather than contrasts with its quality of opulence. Tortoiseshelling can make a feature of anonymous areas such as halls or landings, or highlight details of panelling or furniture. For larger vertical surfaces, it is best to break up the area into regular sections rather than attempt to create an overall pattern.

Novices should think twice before they attempt tortoiseshelling and confine their first attempts to small panels: it requires expertise and practice to make it look stunning.

The traditional colours are warm shades ranging from pale blondes and golden honeys through yellows, reds, browns and blacks. Quite strong colours can be used since the blending process of this technique will soften their impact. Tortoiseshelling is usually done on a yellow ground coat, but a red or green base colour can also produce fabulous and unusual effects. Build the finish up using the same varnishes and colours as prescribed below for a yellow ground.

The essential characteristic of a tortoiseshelled finish is the blurred diagonal. Diagonal streaks of broken colour are floated on a wet varnish and distressed in a criss-cross fashion. The distressing strokes soften and merge the colours, reinforcing the diagonal accent. Tortoiseshelling is difficult to achieve with water-based paints.

Method

Apply one coat of undercoat (thinned two parts paint to one part white spirit) to a prepared surface. When this has dried, cover with a ground coat of eggshell, traditionally sharp yellow in colour, thinned three parts paint to one part white spirit. Allow to dry and then brush on a liberal coat of glossy polyurethane varnish, tinted dark oak and thinned two parts varnish to one part white spirit.

While the varnish is still wet, use a 25 mm (1 in.) flat artist's brush to create broken diagonal squiggles, fidgeting the brush in a zigzag manner to move the varnish over the surface. Place blobs of the same varnish on and between these marks, to accentuate the diagonal.

Mix a burnt umber colour in artist's oils and apply small diagonal squiggles running in the same direction. Repeat the process using black. All the markings should be random and casual. Soften the surface by stroking with a 10 cm (4 in.) dry flat brush across and with the diagonals, finishing with a final, strong stroke in the direction of the original diagonal.

For an even richer effect, repeat the whole process, beginning with the first coat of tinted varnish.

When the finish is dry, seal and protect with two coats clear polyurethane varnish (thinned three parts varnish to one part white spirit).

STENCILLING

Highly versatile, simple and effective, stencilling is a deserved-ly popular decorative technique. Depending on the colours and design, it can be subtle and evocative, or bold and forthright. Stencilling is a repetitive method of applying a design in paint that involves using a cut-out motif as a mask or stencil. Almost any surface, from walls and floors to furniture, can be decorated in this way.

Planning is essential. Colours must be chosen to comple-ment your existing scheme. Especially in the case of stencilled borders, study the proportions of the room and work out the positioning of the design carefully. If you are going to stencil a pattern on the floor, ensure the design will be seen, not covered up by a large piece of furniture.

Ready-made stencils are available from artists' suppliers and craft shops. Most are traditional motifs that come pre-cut and with suggestions for colour combinations. More satisfying is to make your own stencil – it's not difficult to do and is the best way of achieving a truly personal look.

One of the great advantages of stencilling is that patterns can easily be scaled up or down by constructing a grid or using graph paper. In this way, the same motif in different sizes can be used to co-ordinate walls, floors, furniture and even vases and crockery.

Making your own stencil

The first step is to draw up your design on graph paper and colour it in. Then fix the drawing to a flat surface and overlay it with a piece of tracing paper. Trace around all the areas that are in one particular colour. Repeat this process, using separate overlays for each colour. Templates can now be made in acetate film or oil stencil board, both of which are available from artists' suppliers or craft shops.

To make acetate stencils, pin the tracing on to a drawing board and overlay with a sheet of acetate. Trace the pattern on to the film using a drafting pen and cut it out with a craft knife. Repeat until all templates are cut. To make a stencil from oil stencil board, you must first trace off the pattern from the tracing paper. Cut out the stencils with a craft knife, using a steel rule to guide you. In either case, leave a big

Opposite: A lavatory can provide an opportunity for an extravagant effect inappropriate elsewhere. Tortoiseshell would never be used like this, but with paint anything's possible.

Above: Traditionally stencils are used to create an air of rustic charm. Here a stencil evocative of rural simplicity decorates the panels of the door and bath surround.

enough margin to maintain some rigidity in the template, and make sure that you have lined up your registration marks accurately (see below). If a thick material such as cardboard is used, the edges should be chamfered or bevelled to prevent paint from creeping under the stencil and blurring the outline.

Registration

The crucial element in stencilling is getting each colour in exactly the right position relative to the other colours and to the completed designs. One way to do this when stencilling a frieze round the top or bottom of a room, for example, is to position each separation of the design on the card or acetate in such a way that they have only to be jammed up against the ceiling, picture rail, floor or skirting board to appear at a uniform height. This means you will have to cut each piece of card or acetate to the same size in the first place.

Another way is to draw a line across each piece of tracing paper in exactly the same position relative to the design. Transfer this to the card or acetate. Mark up your wall in blue chalk with an unbroken horizontal line to indicate where the

Two friezes, one pretty and pastel, the other bold and dominating, exemplify a very common and effective application of the stencilling technique. On this page, several stencils from one design were combined, reversed and twisted around to produce a lively, softly coloured border. Opposite, the inspiration for the stencil came from the Egyptian print on the wall. One stencil only was needed, incorporating four of the lily shapes, and this was repeated around the room. Gold paint gives a touch of extravagance – as it is rather runny, it is best to dry it out on a saucer for a while before using it. Notice how in both examples the paint was not applied evenly through the stencil but shaded across each part of the design to soften outlines and give an illusion of depth.

stencil should go (you may need several lines if you are repeating the design vertically), and then match the lines on the card or acetate with the line on the wall.

Applying the stencil

Although any type of paint is suitable, fast-drying types such as acrylics are ideal. If you find acrylic paint is too expensive, emulsion makes a good alternative. You can also use wood dyes on floors. To apply the paint, you will also need to invest in a square-ended stencil brush.

Mark your registration line on the surface with chalk. Ensure that any drops are perfectly vertical by using a plumb-line, and that horizontals are aligned with either the ceiling or the floor, depending on which is nearest.

The paint should be thinned to a creamy consistency. Apply a small amount to the tip of the brush and dab or pounce it on to the surface, rolling the brush slightly. The effect can be one of bold, solid colour, or you can pounce the paint in such a way that a soft, graduated effect emerges. The stencil should be held firm and flat, and cleaned and dried regularly to prevent blurred or smudgy edges. Try to blend two or more colours together on one overlay to produce depth and subtlety, and don't feel constrained by the separations of colour on which you originally decided. Be bold and adventurous, and vary and graduate the colours between and within the stencils. Move the stencils around, flip them over, turn them through 90° – you will be surprised at the range of effects you can create.

Stencilling is usually left as a matt finish, but on floors you will need to protect the pattern with five or six coats of polyurethane varnish.

Using aerosols

Aerosols give a flat and even result but the paint has a tendency to spread under the stencil. They are useful on a small scale, or to achieve graduated shading. Cover the surface first with a recommended primer or sealer and then sand lightly before applying the paint. Use the manufacturer's recommended lacquer to protect and seal the surface.

The stencil motif used all over the walls in this room came from a seventeenth-century French fabric design. It was applied over walls washed with a stone coloured glaze, and the yellow, aged effect was achieved by varnishing the entire surface. Below the dado rail, the walls are dragged. The owner's treasures could not have found a richer backdrop.

Stencilling

1. Draw your design to scale on graph paper and colour it in. Draw registration line.

2. Tape a sheet of tracing paper over the drawing and trace around all the areas that are in one colour. Do this for each colour, and trace off the registration line.

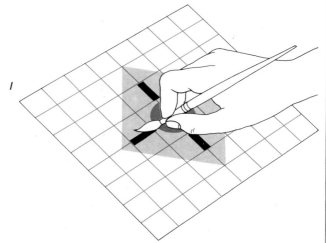

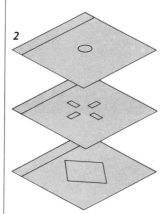

3. Tape each tracing paper overlay over a piece of oil stencil board and trace off the pattern and the line. Alternatively, overlay the tracing paper with a sheet of acetate and trace the pattern on to the film. Score the registration line in the correct place across the acetate.

4. Cut the stencil out of the film or card.

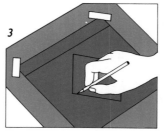

5. Draw a line in blue chalk on the wall where the stencil is to go. Match the line on your stencil card or acetate with this line. Hold the stencil flat, or tape it to the wall, and dab or pounce paint through with a stencil brush.

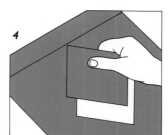

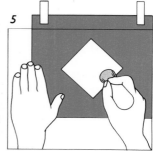

TROMPE L'OEIL

Trompe l'oeil – literally fooling the eye – represents the most ambitious form of illusion. Here the aim is to reproduce a scene so accurately that the spectator is momentarily tricked into believing that it is real. Often whimsical in spirit, *trompe l'oeil* ranges from meticulously rendered views, small masterpieces in their own right, to faked details such as plasterwork decoration or panelling (page 33).

Virtuoso displays are best left to the professionals. Even for the amateur, some artistic ability is required. But *trompe l'oeil* need not be on a grand scale. Unambitious details and visual jokes can be supremely effective – like storage jars painted to look as if they are standing on a kitchen work surface. You can use stencils to help you build up a *trompe l'oeil* – a balustrade, for example, could be very effectively created using just one template – and scaling a stencil design up or down on graph paper will enable you to get perspectives right. For those who still lack confidence, the solution might be to paint a *trompe l'oeil* on a panel, which can then be mounted over a door or in a recess.

Transferring *trompe l'oeil* designs

A simple way to transfer a design, particularly if the wall has a recess, is to project a slide on a wall and draw around the outlines.

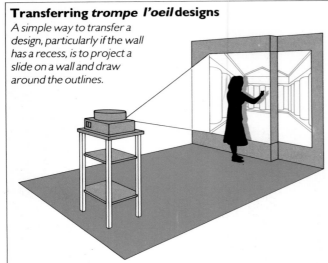

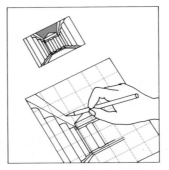

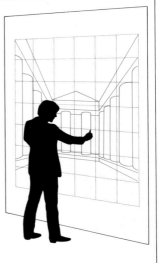

Alternatively, draw your design on to graph paper. Then draw an accurate grid on the wall in blue chalk and transfer the design carefully, square by square.

Left: A trompe l'oeil *urn sits next to a real one in this room. Such visual witticisms can enhance a* trompe l'oeil *or point up the faults in it; here the lush plant makes the joke plain.*

Below: This window really does deceive the eye, as all trompe l'oeil *should. The same idea carried out indoors can make a room feel twice the size, and banish rainy days forever.*

PAINTED FLOORS

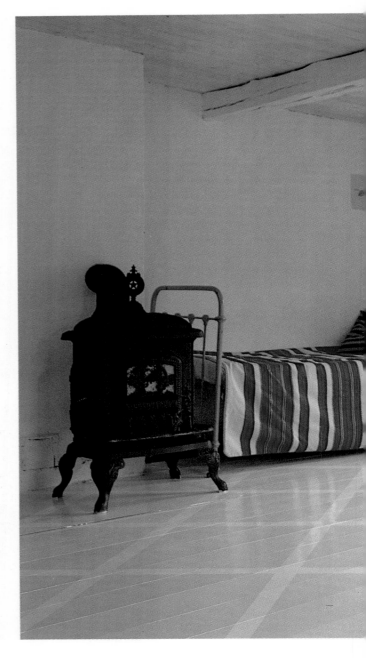

Painting a floor is a cheap, functional and decorative solution that compares favourably with other, more expensive options such as carpeting, tiling and laying linoleum. The scope is wide – from single colour treatments to the bold patterns you can achieve with techniques such as combing and stencilling. Even *trompe l'oeil* is a possibility. Properly sealed, a painted floor will only require a minimum of maintenance and will age gracefully over the years.

Apart from reasons of economy, painting a floor can be a good way of retaining the practical advantages of a wooden surface, such as warmth and durability, without being restricted to a relatively narrow colour range. Depending on the colours and design you choose, the result can be rich and lustrous or bright and cheerful, sophisticated or naïve.

Floorboards, chipboard or hardboard floors are suitable but, as is the case with all painted finishes, the final result depends to a large extent on the structural integrity of the surface and the degree of preparation.

Another drawback is that the room will effectively be out of action for several weeks. This is not only due to the drying time of the painted finish but also because four or five coats of varnish must be applied to protect it. This problem can only be sidestepped by prefabricating a design on chipboard or hardboard and applying it in panels over the existing floor.

The best paints to use on stripped natural wood are wood dyes or stains, although these are not suitable for distressing techniques. The increased popularity of stained floors means that dyes are now available in a much wider colour range than before; or, if you prefer to paint your floor or if you want to create a distressed finish, you can mix up your own coloured paints, tinting undercoat or flat oil with artist's oils.

Making good
Before you start to work, inspect the floor thoroughly to make sure that it is sound, and free from any damage due to

Cool Scandinavian simplicity is powerfully evoked by this interior, dominated as it is by its painted floor in geometric design. It is the simplest of painted floors to copy, provided your floorboards are in good condition: green was painted on to the floorboards, white lines painted over that, and then the surface was finished with a mid-sheen varnish. The room shows that a floor can be the single decorated element in a scheme without any sacrifice of pattern or charm; it can also offer an opportunity to use colours with bold originality, creating a highly personal signature.

rot or woodworm. Secure any loose or squeaking boards with nails or screws. Large gaps or cracks in the floorboards can be filled by wood fillets. They should be thoroughly secured and be of a similar type of wood to the floorboards, so that stains are evenly adopted. Other types of filler will not absorb the paint or stain in the same way as the surrounding wood, so it is best to avoid them. If your design is based on the pattern of the floorboards, proprietary brands of marine sealant can be used between each floorboard, and this will prevent draughts and dust coming up through the floor. Push the sealant between the boards and run a dowel along to push it below the level of the floor.

Prepare for painting by scrubbing the entire floor with hot, soapy water or bleach, and allow it to dry. Knee cap protectors can make the whole job more comfortable!

Stripping and sanding

Stripping a floor is backbreaking work. Luckily, it is only really necessary if the floor is in very bad condition or very uneven, or if the surface finish has been planned to incorporate the natural grain of the wood.

One method is to use an industrial blow torch to burn off old paint or varnish. The whole procedure is unpleasant and strict fire precautions should be observed. The stripped boards will be superficially charred; deep sanding will be necessary to prepare and level the surface.

The most common method of stripping a floor is to use an industrial sander. These can be hired on a daily basis. Take a sample of the floorboards to the hire shop so you can be advised on the best grit of sandpaper to use. Before you start, make sure all repairs are done. Go over the floor with coarse paper, sanding diagonally to the grain. Sand again, this time on the other diagonal. On the next run, use fine paper to sand with the grain. Keep a window open and wear a mask and goggles to prevent inhaling the fine dust. When you've finished sanding, give the floor a thorough clean with white spirit, and ensure all dust has been removed. Dispose of all debris very carefully. Sanding is a very messy business, so should be carried out before any other decorating.

Plain finishes

On natural wood floors that have been sanded and stripped to expose the grain, wood dyes or stains are very effective. These are available in standard ranges of natural wood colours, but also in brighter primary shades. As a rule, a dark wood cannot be lightened with a light stain, so the colour you choose will depend partly on the colour of the existing wood.

It is important to test a stain by applying it to a small area first and leaving it to dry. The colours shown on the tin can be misleading; most dry much darker than indicated.

No primer is necessary. Apply the stain to a clean, dry floor, working towards an exit. You can kneel on a flat board to prevent damage to the surface. After the stain has dried, seal the floor with four or five coats of polyurethane varnish, allowing 12 hours between coats. A simple and very effective variation on this theme is to stain boards in different colours.

An alternative way of colouring floorboards is to use a wash composed of flat oil or undercoat tinted to the desired shade. With this method it is possible to lighten wood, since the paint has a greater covering capacity than stain. If you mix the paint with a small amount of filler, it will smooth over minor imperfections and coarse grain at the same time.

Apply the wash to a clean, dry, sanded surface, working in sections and wiping the boards with a cloth to remove excess paint. The colour will permeate the wood; if you then sand the floor, the grain will be highlighted but the colour will remain in the wood texture. This exposed grain can be left as it is or stained another colour. The finish should be sealed with polyurethane varnish as above.

Creating patterns

Although all the broken colour techniques can be applied to floors, the most successful are those which exhibit the boldest patterns. Combing is particularly effective (page 39), as are spattering and cissing (pages 40-3); but effects which rely on subtlety, like dragging, would just be wasted effort.

Good preparation is essential. Natural wood should first be primed and left for 24 hours. Next, apply an undercoat, leaving it to dry for 12 hours. It is important to allow plenty of

Floors

1. Check over all the floorboards for irregularities, large gaps and holes. Sink nailheads using a hammer and nail punch. Secure loose floorboards effectively.

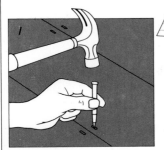

2. Fill cracks or large holes between floorboards by countersinking wooden fillets: cut pieces of wood into appropriately-sized wedge shapes, and hammer home until they fit snugly below the surface of the floor. Make sure they are very secure.

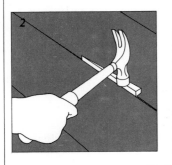

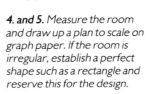

3. Sand the surface with an industrial sander. Sand once diagonally to the grain, then in the other direction. Then sand with the grain. Take proper safety precautions.

4. and 5. Measure the room and draw up a plan to scale on graph paper. If the room is irregular, establish a perfect shape such as a rectangle and reserve this for the design.

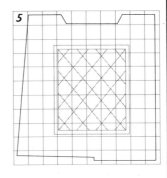

6. Transfer the design to the floor: make straight lines by chalking a piece of string, tying it to two nails and 'snapping' it on the surface.

7. Tie a piece of string to a nail to make a circle; for an oval, use two nails and pull the chalk against the string.

time at this stage since the surface must be able to withstand being walked on during the application of subsequent coats.

For the opaque base coat, tint undercoat or flat oil to the required colour and apply two coats. Emulsion is not suitable. The distressed coat should be thicker than usual (three parts paint to one part solvent). Work in sections approximately 1 metre (3 feet) square. For combing, try out a variety of patterns, perhaps using different combs. Plan ahead by drawing the pattern section by section in chalk. If you want to maintain a clean edge where the patterns meet, mask out adjoining sections with cardboard and masking tape. When the finish is dry, seal with five coats of polyurethane varnish, leaving 24 hours between coats.

Aside from broken colour, patterns can also be created using flat colour, either by stencilling motifs in different dyes or by making a geometric design. Here, the planning stage is very important. Establish the exact dimensions of the room and draw it up on graph paper. Joins between floorboards should be incorporated in the pattern so that lines do not conflict. Most rooms are irregular in shape, so establish a regular rectangle or other perfect shape within the room and treat this as an outline for the pattern, with the remainder of the area left as a border.

Hardboard and chipboard

If the floor is in such a bad condition that a painted finish is impossible to achieve, an alternative is to cover the whole area with hardboard or chipboard. This serves both to exclude draughts and provide a flat, smooth surface.

Hardboard is flexible enough to accommodate a bowing floor, but sharp ridges must be sealed and severe dips filled to prevent the hardboard from splitting. Chipboard is more substantial and is ideal for panelling.

Although these floors can be decorated *in situ*, a design can also be prefabricated on panels so that the room is never out of commission. Work the design out carefully on graph paper and consider how the panels will be fixed so that joins will not be visible when the floor is laid – for example by incorporating the panel joins in the design.

Far left: Staircases are frequently overlooked by the home decorator, who too often falls into the trap of the neutral stair carpet. The staircase may turn out to have a wooden floor in better condition than many rooms, just crying out for a paint finish. These stairs show one original approach. Blobs of dark and light paint in the form of a glaze were applied to a ground colour of a pretty, yellowy grey, then smudged with a dry cloth or brush. A seal of gloss varnish protects against wear and tear.

Left, above: In this kitchen the painted floor has been deliberately left at the mercy of passing feet. A very light blue wash was applied and sanded down lightly. The grain has become prominent where the floor gets most use, and the effect is eventually a pleasing one of age and wear.

Left, below: Stencilling is a favourite for floor decoration. This ragged hallway has the floor as its focus, where a stencil seems to fall down the stairs. It was done simply by repeating one design, cut very intricately, and spraying paint through it with an aerosol.

PREPARATION

There is no substitute for structural integrity – paint can do nothing for rotted wood, corroding metal or crumbling plaster. Applying paint to a poor surface will only result in the swift deterioration of a finish.

Even sound surfaces need to be properly prepared. In general, this involves repairing minor imperfections and making sure the surface is clean, dry and degreased. Most will also need a suitably coloured undercoat to provide a sealing film and facilitate the application of successive coats of paint. New or stripped wood and bare metal must be treated with the recommended primers before undercoating.

Tools

An essential part of good preparation is having the right tools for the job. Apart from specialist distressing tools, basic equipment consists of brushes and rollers. As with paint, you should buy the best you can afford, and take care of them properly when they are not in use. Rollers make fast work of applying ground coats and are excellent for painting ceilings, especially if you attach an extension; it is not advisable to use them with gloss paint since the finish tends to peel off.

Care for your brushes and rollers by cleaning them with the relevant solvent and then rinsing thoroughly in water. Don't stand them upright, hang them up when dry or store overnight in a plastic bag. Decant paint into a paint kettle (for a brush) or a sloping tray (for a roller). Never overload a brush or roller with paint.

Other useful items include ladders and an ample supply of clean dust sheets to protect surrounding areas. A stock of lining paper or sheets of hardboard will enable you to try out different techniques or practise making prints.

Preparing walls

Although some techniques, such as sponging and ragging, are useful for camouflaging minor imperfections, a finish will still only be as good as the initial preparation. Mid-sheen or gloss finishes, in particular, will only highlight unevenness or flaws in the plasterwork.

Plaster or painted walls in reasonable condition should be

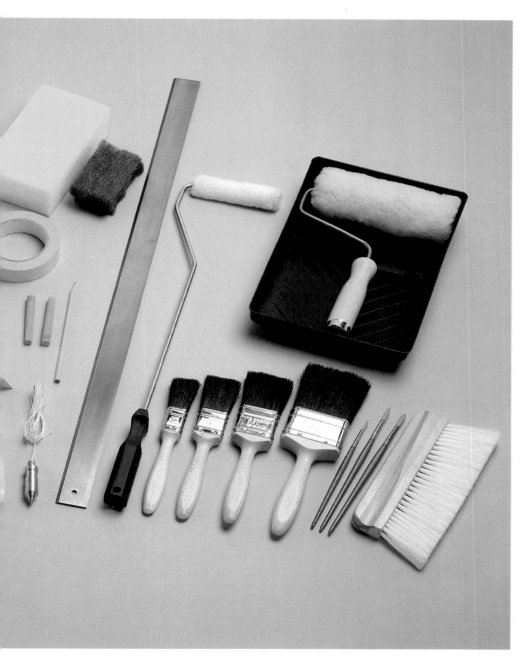

Essential tools (anti-clockwise from top centre): sponge for washing walls; paint kettle; solvents – paint stripper, brush cleaner, etc.; rubber gloves; abrasive papers of different grades; sanding block; Mastic gun for pushing liquid filler into cracks and holes; wallpaper scrapers; shave hooks for stripping paint and varnish from architraves, moulded plasterwork and difficult corners; plumbline; tools for marking out: tape measure, chalks, pencils; steel straight-edger and masking tape; radiator roller, useful for awkward corners and features where an ordinary roller (right) will not reach; assorted paint brushes, including artist's brushes; soft wallpaper brush, useful for 'softening' paint effects.

washed with a mild detergent containing a little bleach or disinfectant. Use a slightly abrasive scourer and wear gloves to protect your hands.

For walls that exhibit shallow cracks or small imperfections, sand the area with glasspaper, then level with a proprietary filler. For deeper cracks see opposite.

If the plasterwork is basically sound but shabby, covering it with lining paper will provide an even surface. Care should be taken to camouflage the joins by butt-jamming the edges.

Stripping wallpaper

Papered walls need to be stripped in order to achieve a satisfactory painted finish. The easiest way is to hire a wallpaper stripping machine from your local DIY or decorating shop. Waterproof paper such as vinyl and anaglypta should be scored with a knife in a criss-cross pattern to allow water to penetrate.

If you don't want to hire a machine, use a proprietary wallpaper stripper, a scraper and plenty of hot water.

Preparing woodwork

Many homes contain a surprising amount of woodwork – mouldings, picture rails, architraves, skirting boards, doors, window frames and dados are all essentially details but still need proper preparation. Since this tends to be a messy business, it should be carried out before walls are tackled.

Stripping paint from wood is tedious, time-consuming, messy and expensive. If possible, avoid it by carrying out local repairs. For small cracks, sand down the area and apply a proprietary filler mixed to a creamy texture, using a brush. Sand the woodwork, especially if it has been painted with gloss, to provide a key for subsequent coats.

If stripping is unavoidable, for example if many layers of paint obscure the lines of mouldings, there are three basic methods you can use. The first is to paint on a chemical paint stripper which acts to soften the paint so that it can be removed with a scraper. This is a slow process and involves the use of strong, caustic alkalis. Read the instructions carefully and always keep a bucket of water on hand to neutralize

any splashes. The advantage of this method is that it can clean small areas heavily clogged with paint without damaging the edges of the wood.

The most versatile paint stripper is a heavy-duty hot air blower. Relatively expensive to hire, it also demands careful use to prevent fire or scorching.

For large accessible areas, such as floors and big pieces of furniture, paint can be removed by sanding with a flat bed random orbital sander or belt sander. The hire charge normally includes paper. The heavy grades of paper (40 grit) will clear off the bulk of the paint but the surface must be sanded again with finer grade paper (80/100 grit) to give a good surface. These machines are heavy to operate and make a good deal of mess. Wear a face mask and goggles to prevent inhaling the dust and dispose of debris carefully.

For basic floor preparation see pages 66-9.

Preparing furniture

How you prepare furniture depends on the fineness of the piece and the finish you intend to apply. Quality antiques need considerable care.

Painted furniture in good condition should be washed with detergent and bleach or disinfectant, using an abrasive sponge. When the piece is dry, undercoat can be applied if necessary. For minor imperfections, sand and fill, priming if the natural wood is exposed.

If the piece is substantially marked, it will need to be stripped. This can be achieved with chemical stripper, a hot air blower or by sending it to be commercially stripped. This involves immersing the piece in a hot caustic dip. With the renewed interest in stripped pine and natural wood finishes, there are many companies that engage in wood refurbishment, and prices are competitive. The process is suitable for any wood that is transportable, including mouldings and doors, but is not advised for fine furniture. Dipped wood should be scrubbed with hot soapy water containing a little vinegar to neutralize any caustic substances still in the grain. After stripping, if the furniture is to be painted, it should be lightly sanded, primed and undercoated.

Preparing walls

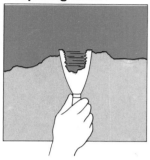 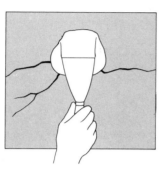  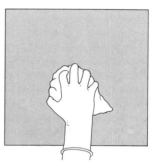

1. Strip off wallpaper by using proprietary stripper, a scraper and hot water; or hire a stripping machine and follow the instructions.

2. Fill large cracks with proprietary filler mixed to a stiff consistency, applying this with a spreader and making sure there are no air pockets.

3. Remove excess with a damp cloth. When the filler is thoroughly hardened sand down lightly for a flat surface without cracks or holes.

4. Whatever repairs you do, wash the walls with mild detergent mixed with a little bleach or disinfectant. Wear gloves and use a scourer.

Preparing woodwork

1. Layers of old paint can be removed with chemical paint stripper. Scrape off the softened paint, taking care not to damage the surface.

2. Alternatively, use a hot-air stripper or blowtorch to burn the paint off. Work from the bottom upwards, and take safety precautions.

3. For small cracks, apply a wood filler, mixed to a creamy consistency. Ready-mixed preparations can be 'injected' with a pump-action 'gun'.

4. Sand filled cracks, then sand the entire surface, especially if the woodwork has been painted with gloss, to provide a key for new coats of paint.

PAINTING PROCEDURE

Once the surface has been prepared, the first coats of paint can be applied. Bare wood or metal require the application of a primer to seal the raw surface. In all cases, an undercoat is also necessary to provide a suitable base for finishes. This can be either water- or oil-based.

Water-based paints will cover any clean, dry and degreased surface, except metal (which will rust). On new plaster, the first coat should be emulsion and thinned (one part paint to one part solvent) to act as a primer. The subsequent coat can be full strength. If you are painting over a dark surface, up to three coats may be required.

The order in which you paint is important: generally speaking, you should start nearest the source of natural light, and paint away from it. Paint the ceiling first and the floor last, and the walls before the woodwork (see opposite). Work systematically, laying off strokes on walls and ceilings in the direction of the light. On woodwork, paint should be laid off in the direction of the grain. Laying off consists of a light finishing stroke intended to obliterate brushmarks.

Straight-edging and masking

Professional decorators, with the co-ordination that comes from experience, can paint straight edges and highlight detail freehand. For the amateur, there are certain techniques that ensure paint goes where it is intended. These are particularly important in flat colour schemes where mouldings, plasterwork or panelling are picked out in different colours.

The simplest and most successful way to get a clean, straight edge is to paint against a chamfered piece of thin, stiff material. When painting a moulding, for example, place the chamfered edge right up against the wood and apply paint sparingly to prevent runs. Move the straight edge along as you paint, wiping any excess paint off with a clean cloth.

Masking out the areas not to be painted is essential, particularly when employing broken colour techniques. A few hours spent masking out all wood surrounds with masking tape will be time very well spent, for you should end up with crisp, clean edges. Take care not to damage the paint when you remove the tape, especially if using emulsion.

Basic painting techniques

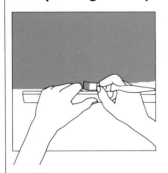

1. Keep a straight edge by running the stock of the brush along a ruler or piece of stiff board held at an angle to the surface being painted.

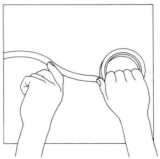

2. When painting a curved shape, mask out surrounding areas with masking tape. Take care not to remove any paint with the tape.

3. Work down the walls in 60 cm (2 ft) sections. 'Lay on' the paint vertically, and use cross strokes to prevent a striped effect.

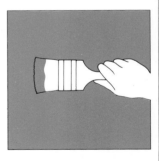

4. The last or 'laying off' stroke should be a light flick with a fairly dry brush across the surface to eliminate any brushmarks.

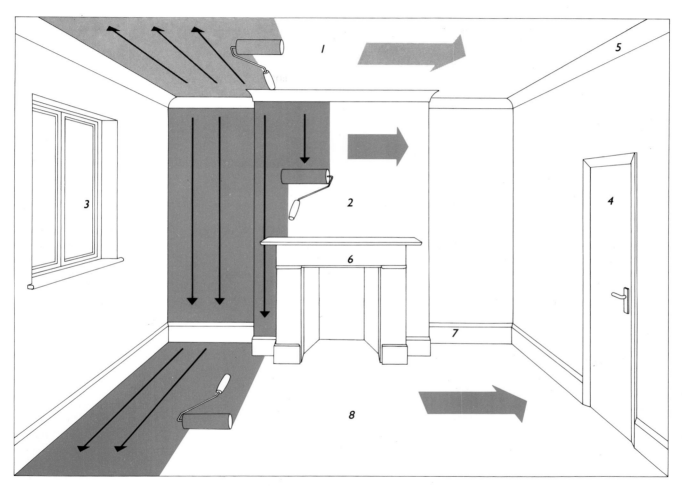

Painting sequence

There is a correct order in which to paint all the elements in a room. First, tackle the ceiling, working in bands away from the main source of natural light (1). Next, paint the walls, again away from the natural light, working in vertical strips 60 cm (2 ft) wide (2). Then paint window frames, starting with the inside of the frame and finishing with the sill (3). For doors, paint panels first, followed by crosspieces and then architraves (4). Next, paint plasterwork details such as cornices and mouldings (5), followed by fireplaces (6). Paint all skirting boards (7). Floors are painted like ceilings, working in bands away from natural light: always work towards an exit (8).

INDEX

Acknowledgments

Illustrators: Mulkern Rutherford Studio.

The publisher thanks the following photographers and organizations for their kind permission to reproduce the pictures in this book:

Abitare (Antonia Mulas) 13; Arcaid/Lucinda Lambton (stencils from Lyn le Grice, Bread Street, Penzance) 59; Jonathan Bartlett (by courtesy Timothy Wright, paint finish by Jonathan Bartlett) 58; Crown Plus Two Colour Cue Range 10, 11; Davies Keeling Trowbridge 53, 54 above; Dulux/ICI 17 below; Lars Hallen 66-67; Good Housekeeping (Jan Baldwin) 71 above; Ken Kirkwood 16 left; La Maison de Marie Claire (Chabaneix/Boyle) 14-15 (Godeaut/Belmont) 17 above (Eriaud/Comte) 40, 64; Bent Rej 65; Jessica Strang 28-29 (Henrietta Green) 51 (stencils from Lyn le Grice, Bread Street, Penzance) 32-33, 71 below; Syndication International/Options 2, 16-17, 35; Fritz von der Schulenberg 70-71; Elizabeth Whiting & Associates (Spike Powell) 24-25.

The publishers are grateful to the following for their help with special photography:

Photography by Simon Brown: Jennifer Taylor 27; architect Ian Hutchinson 31, 41; Paul Hodgkinson 43; François Gilles from I.P.L. Interiors-Paris-London (paint effects by Nick Fer and Michael Snyder) 48-49; Roger Britnell (paint by John Ebdon) 50-51, 54 below; architects de Blacam & Meagher 55; Graham Carr 62-63. **Photography by John Heseltine:** 10-11, 72-73. **Photography by Shona Wood:** Laura Fortescue (colour washing by Penelope Beech) 6-7; Jonathan Bartlett 18-19, 20 right; Holland/Hyatt 20 left, 29 below, 60; fashion designer Stephen King (paint finishes by Jonathan Bartlett) 21, 26; Robert and Colleen Bery 29 above, 61; Penelope Beech 33, 37 left and right, 56; Anthony Paine 36; Michael Snyder (carpentry by Christopher Penfold) 39; Robert and Winberg (shading by Michael Snyder) 45; Susan Prag (paint finish by Michael Snyder) 46-47.